ISBN: 978-1-906669-00-3

Library of Congress subject heading:
Handbooks, manuals, etc.

Published by LDB Publishing

www.ldbpublishing.com

The Ingredients Of A Good Thriller

OR

A Simple Guide to Noir, Cops, Gangsters, Heists and Badasses in Book and Film, and How to Make That Genre Work For You As A Writer

Chris Wood

LDB Publishing
Manchester, England

www.ldbpublishing.com

Contents

Introduction – About This Book

This book is for people who love thrillers and want to get in on the action. If you enjoy reading or watching them, this is for you. This book explores the area in as much detail as space allows. It is both a companion piece and an appreciation, giving insight and breaking down how things work.

For anyone writing a thriller or looking to direct or act in one, then this should be useful to you. It's extra information to draw from with plenty of good examples to refer to. If you're starting off, this is a handy guide.

This is also a guide for those interested in the area. Many people love thrillers, and if you want to see a bit of the machinery – how they work, basically – then you should find this of interest.

(If you're looking for a basic intro, please read the chapter headed "Essentials." Then read the rest. I promise you that makes sense! It will give you a good basic idea of what you need. Then you can consider the rest as extra ingredients, like spices in cooking)

My own experience is as a writer and fan, and I've looked at the genre in a number of smaller parts. These are explored in greater detail. Hopefully this will give pleasure to the fan and some help to anyone more practically involved. If both applies to you, I hope you will find this well worth your time.

There are any number of ways to approach a piece of writing. Of the writers I know, successful and struggling, each has their own way.

This is not intended to be complete.

It is a guide aimed at the curious, the new, the fledgling, the old hand, the afficionado ... basically, anyone interested in the area.

This is intended to be an easy guide and quick rule of thumb. Hopefully it's both interesting to read and practical.

I love thrillers in their many different forms. I have watched and read them by the thousand. Big deal, good for me and maybe it's the same for you. A lot of this is what I'd want to see, while listing what else you might want to include.

So, that aside ... why bother with this?

1. Why not have a handy guide? While none of this is set in stone, it's a good idea to have some rule of thumb. Any rule can be broken, provided certain things remain intact. To use role reversals or to play on expectations requires an understanding of how these things work.

2. You may have missed some of these. Although this isn't comprehensive (that would be 1,000 pages long at least) it covers a fair few possibilities. Plus it's food for thought.

3. It's a source of amusement. This book has anecdotes, insights and breakdowns of detail,

with some great stories.

4.   There are some basic, sound tips for everyone interested in the area. Things I've developed for myself as well as learned from other people. Maybe you'll find some good ideas here, either as a starting point or that last finishing touch, and anywhere in between.

1
Starting Points

Different Types of Thriller – the Genre Broken Down

Thrillers can be divided into a number of different categories. We all like different stories and, to be fair, each can be approached in a variety of ways. A new take on one of these can be breathtaking. Just doing one type very well can be spectacular.

Hopefully this part will be of special interest to anyone with a specific project in mind. Do remember that, as with anything, you can mix and match. Just take parts as they appeal to you, roll them all together and make them your own.

The Ealing classic *The Ladykillers*, for example, could be considered a mix of gangster movie and passing detective. It worked superbly.

The Gangster Story

From the bangers of *Menace To Society* to the old school types of *White Heat*, gangs and their members are a staple of the thriller. There's lots of potential here. Rogue elements, power struggles, jobs gone wrong, a new member, mistrust, betrayal, informing, greed, adultery ... oo, there's plenty to go on here.

Having the main character in an unexpected position can reap dividends. The narrator in *Layer*

Cake is a blue chip guy who wholesales cocaine. He's a normal businessman in most ways. That makes his situation refreshing, and so the criminal element means more.

Any set of criminals means a gangster story. Kill away, have fun.

Naturally, anti-heroes stand strong here. If most of the characters are bad, the difference between acceptable or unacceptable is crucial.

The Cop Story

World weary detectives, homicide inspectors who've never seen anything quite like this (or are just too familiar), rookie cops, beat officers, the take on the world the cop offers can be great.

Unravelling a story from the position of the investigator is a common trick, but there are many varieties of this. Joseph Wambaugh's book *The Choirboys* looks at cop life from the ground floor, and it's a great read. Anyone wanting to feature beat officers should read this.

Some cop movies look at the politics of their world. *LA Confidential* without the corruption and the machinations wouldn't fly. The niceties of cop life can also be useful sources of tension or conflict, not to mention the moral dilemmas that can arise.

The Private Eye Story

The private eye is often a former cop, and probably someone who keeps some company with police. They have a vested interest in cases and often know the talk and the routine.

A private eye will often have different morals and a varied outlook to a cop. But private eyes vary. Is yours honest? Are they out for justice, or just to get paid? Do they stay loyal to the client? If they're offered money to betray the client's interests, will they?

Another important question is the client. Are they innocent people wronged? Criminals? Have they an ulterior motive (many clients do in these stories)? Will they turn criminal later? Is the investigator looking into a private matter or a commercial crime?

Bear in mind all these elements can lead to so many different things.

The Serial Killer Story

As mentioned elsewhere, there are different types of serial killers in real life, so use this. Vary the traditional expectation – each actual case is different. Read some details and see if anything stands out. Finding some new angle is useful, but what is your actual story?

There are many ways of being grotesque, but original cruelty is rare. In some real crimes there isn't much shortage of this, so if you're writing about this area, look there.

Serial killers aren't always seen as monsters. The unassuming killer, the one nobody has a bad word for, is especially creepy. Bear in mind that when Dennis Nilsen, slayer of 15, was captured, press photographers had to angle their flashlights into his glasses to make him look sinister. He was just so ordinary.

The Whodunnit Story

Fairly self explanatory, this one. Either keep everyone guessing or make the killer known at once and then keep the other characters in suspense. Bear in mind that if we think we know who the killer is, this can be great territory to throw twists into.

The situation is the key here. Find some way that the death is important for unusual reasons. Throwing in a variety of points of intrigue can be useful – sex, jealousy, money, revenge, blackmail, theft, a warning and plain old nuttiness covers most things.

Try not to overdo the red herrings or murkiness. We want the audience to have some way of latching on to the right points of intrigue.

The Heist Story

The 'heist gone wrong' story is overdone, but a new take can always work. Is the condition of the robbery unique? Are the people doing the stealing?

Is there something private going on to twist everything? Does someone have a naughty secret?

A major crime is accompanied by plenty of tension. Criminals are sometimes incontinent on raids (seriously – some burglary scenes clearly show the criminals were very tense), and danger and discovery can effect people in very different ways. Approaching the crime is also a fruitful area to look at. Is there a job being planned? Put together? Explained? Financed? Offered? Sought? Analysed afterwards?

A 'heist goes well' story is rare. After all, your characters can have things go wrong elsewhere.

The Passing Detective Story

It's been said before, but Miss Marple must be the world's worst travelling companion. Anywhere she goes, this likeable lady is followed by a truckload of dead bodies. Gangster films often have a lower body count than this elderly spinster visiting an old friend in the country.

This may seem unlikely, and it is when done to death (no pun intended). Having someone seem like a regular nobody who then turns bloodhound can be most effective, though.

So what makes a good detective? An eye for clues and detail, a feel for people and events, the ability to spot that telling loose strand ... there can be many things about a situation that brings out the surprising sleuth who weaves through the evidence and finds the culprit.

Plots

A plot powers a story like an engine powers a car. Without a plot, people will only pay attention if there is stunning dialogue, or some tremendous action, overwhelming sex appeal or any other compelling element.

Basically, you need a plot.

Some great thrillers have several plots. I mean, a lot can go on in some stories. Below is a variety of approaches, and I'm not saying any of them is right. This is food for thought – if anything leaps out, grab it and make it your own.

Firstly, are there *really* only seven plots?

Yes, here is a list of seven (different) plots. Other people have broken this down in different ways, but here is a healthy start. Have a look and decide for yourselves.

It's All About People ... Flawed People

Naturally, there's the seven deadly sins (not just for *Se7en*). These can be interpreted as religious or more general human failings.

Gluttony, Greed, Lust, Pride, Sloth, Wrath and Envy

Wanting It All ...

1 – Greed – people want money = trouble. *The Getaway. Bound. No Country For Old Men. Point Blank. Fargo.* This is anything where getting rich is the main motivation.

2 – Gluttony – people want far too much. *Goodfellas. Wall Street. Citizen Kane. Chinatown. Fitzcarraldo.* As greed is more money, gluttony is more general excess. *Scarface* and *Leaving Las Vegas* have that in common.

Assuming that gluttony doesn't just mean cash, we can certainly include *Patton: Lust For Glory.* Or have I spoken too soon?

I Just Need That ...

3 – Lust – when people do things for the object of their desire. *The Great Gatsby* is one example, as Jay Gatsby without his love for Daisy would just be another city crook. There's also the fuller definition, whereby some love or lust pulls people away from their duties. Al Pacino in *Heat*, letting another family fall apart as he chases his prey. It isn't sexual lust, but lust for the hunt that keeps him on the job and estranged.

More regular examples of lust can be found in *9 1/2 Weeks* and *Natural Born Killers.* One is lust for sex, the other for violence. Anything in between, or even over the boundaries of these two films, may be considered lust.

The above three are crimes of excess, and in some degree interchangeable. They are very similar, let's face it. All the protagonists in *Reservoir Dogs* are guilty of one of the above, as even cop Tim Roth has a lust to succeed. How they respond later helps define their characters.

Do remember that you can mix and match these elements as you choose, and this can be an easy way of keeping an eye on who's doing what.

Moving On From Excess

The remaining four deadly sins are as follows:

I'm The Best, I'm The Best!

4 – Pride – here you can put any story with a self destructive type who damages themselves sooner than back down. *The Royal Tenenbaums. Amadeus. Pollock. Shine.* Helen Mirren in *The Queen.* Even *Heat* – De Niro would've gotten away without that last detail to attend to. Or those pesky kids (sorry).

You can fit *The Wild Bunch* in here. If those guys had ignored Angel's death, they'd have survived – but not been very wild. You can also include *Chinatown*, because if Jack Nicholson had walked away, the film would've been happier, at least for him.

Supposing It's What You Don't Do?

5 – Sloth – when people sleep through movies? Ho ho, only kidding. Let's say that sloth here means neglect – of loved ones, dependents, values, places, crafts ... like when Joe Pesci kills a made guy in *Goodfellas*, and ensures his own death. It also sums up John Huston in *Chinatown*, ignoring traditional family values to a startling degree. Notice how *Chinatown* crops up repeatedly? Just goes to show how one great film can combine many different strands.

In early Christianity sloth meant sadness, so any story about wallowing in emotions would qualify here as well.

It Just Makes Me Mad!

6 – Wrath – any revenge flick, so *The Wrath of Khan* would have to serve as an example, I'd say. *Point Blank* certainly qualifies, as does *Foxy Brown* and any number of stories about vengeance.

They All Have It, But I Want It!

7 – Envy – wanting to bring someone down because of something they have. *Cape Fear* would have to qualify here, as well being as a revenge drama. There's also the murderous *Heathers*, whose insecurity and envy fuels their crimes.

Naturally these plots centre around individual failings, but so many stories do. Shortly before I wrote this Sir Edmund Hillary, a great man, died. Had his expeditions ended in failure rather than glory, he would have featured in one of the above. As he succeeded, what category features his story?

An interesting adjunct to the list above would be how many great films and books have been ruined by directors / writers / studios / editors / actors / whoever messing things up due to human weakness. But that would take forever and thousands of pages.

The above list is about weakness, naturally – what makes us human. But some stories are more than that, or not even about such things directly, if at all. But as an underlying approach, the above is pretty good.

Settings

Can Thrillers Happen Anywhere?

Well, where do thrillers happen? Where do thrilling things happen?

That's a fairly open way of saying anywhere, as anything is possible. Okay, fair enough, let's look at two real life incidents.

1 – Two youths (for which read complete bastards) threatened me with a machete when I was 17. I was petrified. They rested it on my shoulder about two inches from my neck. I was paying complete attention to them, believe me, even though they were younger and smaller than me. This happened in the park near where I grew up, which was a pleasant place as a rule and full of cheerful people walking dogs and so forth. Frightening things can happen anywhere.

2 – A man was murdered down the road from me. Same area; no, not Beirut, but some teenagers broke into his flat to steal his motorbike. They thought he'd be unconscious as he was a heavy drinker. He was awake, they panicked, one hit him in the neck with a bat.

What I want to convey here is the ordinariness of it. One of these incidents was fatal, the other resulted in no physical harm but a lot of swearing afterwards. To be able to show regular life going on in and around whatever else happens is a supreme skill. Here are several fine examples, with a quick look at each.

Using The Everyday Places

Pulp Fiction, Butch Coolidge getting his watch back

Bruce Willis is annoyed with his girlfriend and it shows. He drives around tense, gritting his teeth, then pulls up and sneaks into the apartment complex. The back yards and fences look extremely normal. So does the complex and Butch's flat, all except the machine gun on the counter and the hitman in the toilet. Nowhere's perfect.

Slightly later, there is the humdrum of a red light, when Marcellus notices Butch. The traffic, the gawkers and the comments all mark this out as a very everyday scene. The smash and chase to follow are all way out of character for this particular stretch of LA. This beautifully contrasted scene makes us very unwary of what lies ahead for them both in the pawn shop.

Using The Everyday Job

The Terminator, Sarah Connor working as a waitress

Okay, story so far – killer robot, back in time, targets all namesakes, human protector, fate of humanity – check. Next we see Sarah arrive late for work, get orders wrong, have kids spoon ice cream into her apron, she knocks things over, people get cross – all very realistic and perfectly ordinary. We suspect this harmless life won't last for very long, and it's all the worse when Arnie pops up blasting disco dancers. On the plus side, it was the 80's.

Using The Everyday Acquaintance

Leon, the polite old building guy

The one who lets Natalie Portman take in her violin and fill out the forms. He really is a sweet fellow, taking a pleasant, unobtrusive interest in the new arrivals. There are some very cheery exchanges between he and Leon, as he mistakenly assumes the latter is her father. When things hot up for the pair, and Matilda announces they are lovers ... his expression is a picture.

Incidentally, slightly later when this fella is telling Jean Reno to sling his hook, he calls him 'Mr MacGuffin' – a beautiful reference (a MacGuffin is a term for the bog standard, gets you from A to B plot device).

The Ingredients Of A Good Thriller

Using The Everyday Scene

Brighton Rock (Graham Greene), the holiday mood at the beginning

In between all the trappings of a 1950's holiday resort, there is a man in deadly fear. While the day trippers eat candy floss and drink ale, a cheerful, tipsy woman makes his acquaintance, unaware of his dread. As the day rolls along, Ida innocently wonders after his health. Then the man is murdered, in as cold and foul a contrast as possible. This is a beautifully judged start, a scene setting mix of fun and death.

Using The Everyday Routine

The Killer Inside Me (Jim Thompson), breakfast at the start

Big, slow, friendly Lou Ford eats his pie and notices a newcomer in town as he finishes his coffee and lights a cigar. He doesn't carry a gun and his conversation is relaxed and easy. He talks like the thoughts take a while to get clear in his head. He's also a very sick individual, but you'd never know from the picture presented at the start.

Having considered these, it is clear that there's umpteen ways of showing the everyday, and charging it with something sinister to give the audience an extra jolt.

Starting Points

What's Traditional?

However, there are traditional settings for a thriller. The police station, the crime scene, the sleuth's home (probably an apartment suffering from neglect, or maybe the opposite – a closely tended family home full of innocence), possibly the villains' hang out, some neutral space like a bar where the characters go to mull over the plot and have a couple of drinks after a tough day.

What's New?

Wherever you set your story, do something new. In *Hard Boiled*, not the subtlest film, Chow Yun Fat hangs out in a jazz bar, where he plays the clarinet (like every bad assed pistol god). In *The Killer*, his meeting point for his contact is a church, iconically used at the end.

So there's two approaches there – go with the familiar, differently, or go with the unexpected (hitmen and churches?) for the age old.

Take What You Know To Make Things Real

Throwing in personal observations from your life and experiences will make things more realistic. Even if you're writing about the way soup congeals or the local bus service, if it's worked in appropriately, it makes the scene more realistic.

Most of the examples given – from *The Terminator*, for example – are just regular slices of ordinary life worked in to make everything seem real. This is exactly how to build credibility.

Crime Scene

The Expected

There are some great jokes in *The Naked Gun* about various silly ways chalk outlines of bodies can appear – dancing, juggling etc. This plays on a cliché, as many movie crime scenes look exactly the same. Either you take that as read and move on – it's just going to be chalk outlines and yellow police tape – or see how this can be used to your advantage.

The Sinister

The Usual Suspects constantly refers back to the crime scene, 27 bodies and a burned out boat. It's sinister and mysterious, and also cries out for an explanation, because how the hell did that happen?

The crime scenes in *Se7en* are individually warped and morbid. An inventive, sadistic mind is at work (either the killer or the writer / director, you decide). Each is a scene of schlocky, noir art and reflects the sin in question. Greed is found in a big corporate law office, gluttony in a shut in's kitchen, lust in a brothel and so forth. Personalising what is done is a good step toward making a classic.

The Ingredients Of A Good Thriller

Take It Where You Want

Crimes can happen anywhere. If you can think of a surprising place for something bad to happen, go for it – what we don't expect (and who thinks they're going to be mugged in, say, a church?) gives us a bigger jolt.

To have a holy statue violated with obscene, even Satanic daubs gives an early shock in *The Exorcist*. A nun raped in a church gives *Bad Lieutenant* a special level of disgust. A rooftop with a rifle shell casing and a ransom note gives *Dirty Harry* a distinctive start.

Make It Count

Sometimes the sheer over the top quality can mark a crime scene as memorable. While it's more horror than thriller, Wes Craven's *Shocker* has a fantastically gruesome murder scene. It's memorable, striking and a fine example.

The hero finds his girlfriend dead. The reveal works back from a blood smeared door frame, then a message in blood written on the mirror (of a 'happy birthday' nature, pleasantly enough). The hero walks in – we can see blood smears over the entire room, then the shot pulls back to his girlfriend's corpse in an immensely bloody bath.

Such an approach works well because it's graphic, striking and excessive, while playing each particular part of the scene for maximum effect like a good card player. Unsurprisingly it's the work of a maestro horror director. Even though we know what's happened (made implicit in the build up), it's still shocking.

Build Those Reactions Up

A good precursor to the crime scene is the reaction of those attending. To have the sleuth walk up and find seasoned cops shocked sends a message to the audience. How is this so bad? Surely in that line of work, nothing shakes you. To suggest something beyond this gives the crime a power that holds special sway over us.

Throw In Something New

Taking a new approach to a crime scene can work wonders for tension. *Manhunter* has the great device of having a gifted, almost preternaturally inciteful investigator feeling out the killer's psychology from his hideous crime scenes. These involve whole families dying.

The detective places himself in the murderer's position, attempting to relive the terrible acts from his perspective and understand his feelings. This jeopardises his sanity, not surprisingly, while giving the crime scenes tremendous added scope.

This fantastically original approach shows the benefits of good – in this case outstanding – source material. The novel *Red Dragon* succeeds handsomely because the psychological elements are handled so well.

They are suggestive and concern such fearsome crimes, proving a fine example of leading the audience's imagination to some hideously dark places and leaving it there to fester. It's eerie – evocative, sinister, and terrifically effective.

How To Play Your Hand

As in many areas in this genre, there are two ways of playing the crime scene card. Either let it go past as exactly what might be expected (officials, areas taped off and so forth), and move on quickly. Or, do something to make the audience take a step back. Something that makes you say to yourself, "What the hell happened there?"

Making The Most and Knowing When To Move On

The idea of playing cards should be taken a little further here. If your way of doing a particular scene or plot point isn't so outstanding, maybe it doesn't need to be. Move on quickly to something that does have an impact. There are plenty of outstanding thrillers where some elements are exactly as you would expect them. This can be used to your advantage if one mundane approach is followed by something very new or strongly different. Ask yourself, which are the strongest cards in your hand, and how can I play them best?

A Good Start Works Wonders

Like Getting Off On The Right Foot ...

A strong beginning can make a world of difference. Many thrillers kick off with the juice straight away, with little by way of preamble. While some stories are best slow boiling, an immediate piece of action can work wonders.

Dirty Harry does this superbly. The cold, loathsome death of a young woman – accompanied by appropriately creepy music and a sinister sense of pace – is soon followed by Harry's mid-lunch gunfight.

By ten minutes in the director has told us that the bad guy is a sick little bastard and the cop following him is more than capable of dishing out trouble. As such, we know we're going to be entertained – and we're interested.

What Grabs The Attention?

A good start doesn't have to mean violence. A piece of tremendous intrigue will do just as well. A lot of thrillers start with what appears to be an ending, only to let the rest of the story flow once the audience knows what one of the mains questions is. *The Usual Suspects* scores well here – we find out straight away that Keyser Soze is a key figure, and that the movie involves surprise, betrayal and death.

Start Off Regular ...

One of the best aspects of Hitchcock's storytelling is to let an ordinary scene turn sinister in the blink of an eye. To line things up that way, and have enough in place for the audience to suddenly realise the situation with one well placed reveal is a great skill.

Hey, That Shouldn't Be Like That ...

Equally, some particularly good detail can accomplish the same effect. Just enough to whet our appetites and keep us curious. Something sufficiently out of place to have people latching on and contructing theories as to why it's like that.

And There's Always ...

In case some gigantic inspiration doesn't strike, a well placed death or piece of action works wonders.

2
Characters

Characters – Overview

This is a simple overview of the different roles a thriller needs. Each of these can be done in a wildly different number of ways. It can be played safe in a go by the numbers way, or hit out wildly with a whole new approach. Wild cards can work fantastically. You can take an apparent cliché and turn it right around.

Traditions

There's nothing wrong with the more traditional approach, either. The main thing is to make characters that the audience can accept. If something seems drastically wrong, it's likely that character won't be accepted. What is needed is an approach that allows your story to be told – and enjoyably, too.

There is a rich variety of characters to use in a thriller, and we're going to look at some of the most popular as well as some of the more oddball. There's no point saying one is better than another – such things are personal. Strong writing or performing can make the everyday seem very new and exciting.

As ever, nothing is set in stone, but as a starting point, here goes.

The Sleuth

Basically ...

This is the main mod, cop, detective, friend in the right / wrong situation or whatever else. The sleuth can be a hero or a sleaze, a pinnacle of morals or complete lowlife. We just need a brain, some understanding and a need to resolve events.

Type Of Person

This area is wide open. The sleuth can be a criminal trying to piece things together (Lee Marvin in *Point Blank*, Michael Caine in *Get Carter*). It can be a patsy being strung along (Jack Nicholson in *Chinatown*), or a cop breaching his own standards (*Dirty Harry*), or perhaps a woman being set up (Jamie Lee Curtis in *Blue Steel*).

Maybe the sleuth is an old lady with a nose for clues (Miss Marple), or an aloof intellectual (Sherlock Holmes), perhaps even a gang of whacky kids and a talking dog (Scooby Doo, but that's pushing it).

Basically, anything you can think of.

Motivation

Getting to the bottom of things is the main reason for a sleuth to draw breath. This can be for justice, professionalism, reward, revenge, curiosity, satisfaction, to win a bet, impress the neighbours, you name it.

It just needs to be relentless and unquestionable. Or does it? Nothing so sharpens the audience's thirst for justice as the prospect of the villain getting away with it. An indifferent sleuth (either genuinely or apparently), such as Holmes in *The Hound of the Baskervilles*, makes the reader salivate ... what if this is the perfect crime? What if the villain goes unpunished? It's an appalling thought, and like many appalling thoughts, very compelling.

Manners And Characteristics

As varied as it gets. Polite, genteel, caustic, stressed, passive, aggressive, thoughtful, plaintive, purposeful, obsessed ... some sleuths appear sloppy (Colombo), others respectful, some even cowardly (Morse hated blood and violence, things many other sleuths thrive on). If your sleuth is physically passive, a sidekick to cover that area is a good idea.

Characters

Eccentricities

Many a good detective craves some weird and wonderful concoction of lifestyle requirements in order to achieve the necessary focus.

Holmes had his violin, Morse his beer and Kojak a lollipop. Dirty Harry couldn't think straight without a gun the size of a howitzer to aid his mental process.

Miss Marple would cheerfully contemplate the ghastliest deeds from behind a pot of tea and a plate of obscenely delicate cakes. Hercule Poirot required a faceful of good cheese, and it's hard to imagine Colombo finding the killer whilst wearing only an anorak.

The field is especially open here. You name it and, with the right amount of panache, audience curiosity and confidence on the author's part, the sky really is the limit.

The Sidekick

Basically ...

Often to cover plot points and ask "Why this?" Some detectives appear psychic. One term for this is "deus ex machina," literally "god out of the machine," or more simply, the sleuth appears to have read the ending. To the more human reader, the sidekick asks what the hell's going on from a plot perspective.

Type Of Person

Holmes had Watson, a retired army surgeon who sometimes takes up private practice. Poirot had Hastings, a former army officer and Dupin had the anonymous narrator of his stories, a gentleman friend and literary scholar. More recently, Scarpetta had Marino, who serves that role as a busy, cynical cop.

The sidekick needs to be loyal, although probably less intelligent and motivated than the sleuth, although this can be twisted around. Often the sidekick is a police partner, someone to do donkeywork and provide backup. The more interesting ones have a connection to the sleuth that is personal and goes beyond business.

Motivation

This is either professional, as in a cop or investigator of some form, or personal, because the sleuth or victim is a friend. Whatever their involvement, this is a person who wants matters resolved.

The sidekick needs some chemistry with the sleuth. This can be either complimentary or antagonistic, provided their fundamental qualities are not compromised.

You can't expect a busy sleuth to cover all the options. Often, a sidekick will arrive with reinforcements when the sleuth's in trouble. Hopefully, the audience will have forgotten their existence in all the excitement and find this a surprise. This is very helpful, especially in keeping our sleuth from meeting a sticky end.

Manners And Characteristics

The sidekick often makes the sleuth look better, just as movie stars often have ugly co-stars to emphasise their own good looks. So the sidekick is unlikely to be any great shakes at whatever they do, unless they excel at something that compliments and does not overshadow the more dominant role the sleuth plays.

Characters

Eccentricities

Likely to be few, if any. While the sleuth can have idiosyncracies all over the place, the sidekick often has to look more regular and stable by comparison. They are the calm around the storm of the main detective, and exist to play second fiddle – no overshadowing allowed.

The sidekick can play a variety of roles:

Comic Relief

Some incarnations of Watson (such as Nigel Bruce) are required to bumble about and make the whole proceedings more tolerable. Many sidekicks do this, and whether it works depends on the tone of a piece.

Bullet Fodder

A little darker, this. Dirty Harry, in particular, had a variety of partners to help with minor details and often to be blown away. This provides drama, action, a call to revenge and of course, helps the main character look better – they don't get wasted.

Narrator

Where would so many thrillers be without Chuckles the Hapless Enabler pointing out that it was in December and snowing, that the dowager was clearly terrified, that never before had such a situation presented itself etc.

In short, without sidekicks, so much of what the sleuth does would go without explanation. As we, the audience, are obviously lacking the know-how as to why certain things are being done, it's often down to the reliable sidekick to provide the right information. Done skillfully, this device can be near invisible – like good acting.

The Villain

Basically ...

There are two types of villain:

The Incredible Nasty
The Understandable Nasty

The Incredible Nasty

More evil than Satan cackling away over his soul collection (not the kind with Aretha Franklin), the Incredible Nasty relishes evil and enjoys it the way some savour fine wine. At their best, the Incredible Nasty can convincingly roll their eyeballs at the sheer vileness of it all, lurking in the darkness with ice for blood and a thirst for pain. Done right, this is great stuff.

Type Of Person

There's got to be something very bleak in their hearts. It may be some form of mental illness, or the result of former abuse ... perhaps we never find out. Maybe just one of those people who is vile through and through. This type of villain does have to be evil, however – just plain bad to the bone.

Manners And Characteristics

Some characters are completely lacking in scruples and it's obvious their malignance is clear. Others hide beneath some façade – the ones we don't expect, who don't seem capable of such terrible things.

This is where clichés can work in your favour. There is something decidedly chilling at the way some apparently twee, harmless souls can work out. One of Agatha Christie's most shocking (for me, anyway) books has a killer who ... biffed an old lady on the head with an axe so she could ... open a refined tea shop! True. And a real eye popper. Axe murderers shouldn't have ambitions to work in catering, surely.

The commonplace can be creepy, and a few twists of the everyday and familiar can make all the difference.

One of James Ellroy's most heartless villains (which is saying something), Dudley Smith, is often to be found playing the stage Irishman. You know, the friendly sort everyone likes. We could consider that in a number of ways, but I doubt it would suggest the catalogue of heartless brutality this arch bastard unleashes over a bloodsoaked trilogy. The movie *LA Confidential*, while superb, barely scratches the surface.

One crime author, Jim Thompson, is both highly regarded and hugely neglected. His book *The Killer Inside Me* is a real chiller, and the narrator, Lou Ford, gleefully works the foulest of deeds all over the place. Whilst being a well liked sheriff and all round nutter.

One of the best bad guys for sheer psychotic villainy is Scorpio in *Dirty Harry*. This feller is made of evil; he breathes evil, smells evil, bathes in evil ... you name it. An oily, repulsive sadist to the fingertips. Anything along these lines is likely to be a good idea, and to attempt such a bastard in your own work is to slice a portion off sheer nastiness (and evil). Incidentally, Andy Robinson, who plays Scorpio, is an ardent pacifist. If you look closely, you can see him flinch slightly every time he fires a gun, as it upset him (he hates guns). Now, that's acting!

Eccentricities

Hatred, greed and madness can be powerful motivators. The scope for personal touches while these pursue their paths is as wide open as it is in real life crimes.

I would suggest being careful about consistency, though. If someone is ruled by a particular set of needs or desires, it must be maintained. A moody loner won't turn sociable just to help the plot. If you're dealing with psychosis, it has to run all down the line.

The Understandable Nasty

Some crimes come from situations that make the actions understandable once the background is known. This doesn't necessarily justify the behaviour, but it at least lifts it away from simple degeneracy.

Type Of Person

This villain has some good reason, however slight, for their foul deeds. While this may sound like not a lot of fun, there are some good elements to play with here.

Motivation

Greed is one of the oldest motives. I'm not saying this is a good reason for murder, but if people kill for revenge, fun, advancement, to cover other murders and so forth, killing for wealth is, well, less evil than, say, killing for some other reasons. Or is it?

The protagonist in *Crime and Punishment* kills a vicious old money lender, to improve the world and so he can use her wealth for good. He considers he can perform such a deed without consequence. His name (Raskolnikov) derives from the Russian for 'schism.' Sadly, he has to kill an innocent person, goes bonkers, confesses and is redeemed after being condemned.

The book is great fun and a ton of giggles. I haven't read it. I got to page 27 and put it to one side, fearing that I would go postal (and wouldn't that be ironic, ho ho). Life's too short.

Some crimes come from an understandable desire for revenge. The victims had done some terrible wrong which, in hindsight, they needed to answer for. This is often unknown throughout most of the drama, making the crime(s) more sinister and the solution somehow understandable. Conan Doyle uses this, and in one tale (*Charles Augustus Milverton*) makes Holmes an accessory to cold blooded murder because of it. Dramatic, no?

If an audience finds the deeds are, in some way, justifiable, they are in a malleable position. Just what is acceptable? What would we do? Could you blow the whistle on someone taking certain types of revenge? Would you feel bad if they got caught?

Shakespeare wrote *Mercy is not itself, that oft looks so / For pardon is still the nurse of second woe* (Measure For Measure), suggesting that to let someone off is inviting them to reoffend, and any innocent suffering is your fault. Concepts of justice often emerge in thrillers, so why not play with them?

The Victim

Basically ...

In certain types of thriller – the whodunnit, for example, or a revenge drama – the identity of the victim is a key part of the whole. Perhaps the sleuth has to work back from the victim's identity to establish who has committed the crime?

At the same time, don't forget the vast potential for red herrings that investigating someone's past can present. Maybe that affair or illicit business deal isn't actually connected to the real motive, but has us guessing away as we consider such angles. Audiences love intrigue. If you have a corpse, or a missing person, having some good juicy elements can make us hugely interested in the victim irrespective of the rest of the plot, and that can make for an excellent story.

Before we can proceed much further, we have to ask ourselves a simple question, "What crime has the victim fallen foul of?"

Kidnapping

Not all kidnap victims are rich, or from wealthy families. Perhaps the kidnapping is intended to make someone hand over an item or perform a task? Perhaps the victim is taken by mistake?

Some kidnapping stories hardly feature the kidnappers, others show them in plenty of detail. *Fargo* and *Raising Arizona* deal with extremely different types of kidnappings, and show plenty of ways such a story can be handled. The underrated *The Way of the Gun* has two desperado types kidnap Juliette Lewis, who is carrying the child of a ruthless billionaire who sends all manner of killers after them. This situation in itself sets the scene for a great piece of action cinema.

Murder

I've mentioned elsewhere the main motivations for murder. If someone has been murdered, ask yourself how much their identity matters for the story to work.

If the victim is dead at the start, we can learn plenty about them from their position in life and what people say. It is a well established device to have plenty of minor characters that all have a different take on the victim, ranging from those who despise them to that one person with something good to say. Perhaps other people's perception of the victim explains why they were killed?

If there is an (apparently) obvious motive for a killing, remember that keeping some hidden elements back for the ending can add extra layers of intrigue. To reverse this, having everyone suspect what has really happened at the start can then lead to twisting the audience's expectations by introducing a red herring which distracts us from the reality of the crime. Remember that whatever is believable is the right way to go here. Audiences like a good ride for their money.

Robbery

Some robberies are extremely commonplace, others involve the theft of a rare (even unique) item. *The Maltese Falcon* is a story that is layered with possibility and suspicious customers, and personally speaking I was in the dark throughout that movie as to what had really occurred. Reading Dashiell Hammett's original novel throws up some great lessons about pointing the reader in the wrong way – again, reading this gives some fine examples of how to handle such material.

Other robbery stories can simply be a way of involving intrigue. The mass murder at the Nite Owl in *LA Confidential* is presented as being a robbery gone wrong, but there are many strands that take the story a long way away from here. If you're wondering how to get your plot going, a simple robbery that leads to many other matters is a good way forward, especially if the main character is a cop.

Type Of Person

A victim can be anybody. Do we get to know the victim before the crime has taken place? Some stories have a corpse at the start that, by the end, we feel we know quite well. Often there are flashbacks involving a murder victim that allow us to see more of their life and the plot centring around them.

If the victim is alive, study the likely responses. If the victim is hiding something, they may well seem either enthusiastic to help the police (and thus distract suspicion) or highly reluctanct to be questioned. We can also see a lot about them from other people's reactions. Do their family, friends or neighbours seem hesitant when certain issues arise?

Motivation

In being robbed or killed? That lies elsewhere. If the victim has done something to provoke this action, that needs to be shown.

Manners And Characteristics

The opinion of friends, family, the neighbours, business partners etc can be highly useful in terms of forming an impression of the situation. These can be misleading or used to give greater background. A good understanding of the victim can be very helpful in involving the audience, especially if they are either wholly innocent or in some way corrupt, such as complicit in crimes elsewhere.

Murder On The Orient Express has a victim that, on the face of it, is the height of respectability. Once the conclusion becomes known, however, we see that most of the other characters have been involved in the man's death, and for a variety of good reasons.

The kidnap victim in *Fargo* is a wife and mother who is completely blameless. We see her in everyday life – she's not particularly dynamic but still wholly undeserving of her fate. When she is kidnapped, apart from the perfectly reasonable shock reaction, she is a form of comic relief and there to complicate the kidnapping. Her final fate is shocking and underlines one of the criminals as completely homicidal.

Eccentricities

Remember that people are surprisingly varied. We may expect, for example, a wealthy landowner to be haughty, but they could be down to earth and approachable. Similarly someone in an official role may just be doing that as a day job until they can fulfil a dream, such as opening a restaurant or setting up as a tattooist. What surprises the audience helps add, in a variety of forms, to the tension.

The Sleuth's Impression

Quite often the investigator has, for whatever reason, a pre-formed impression of the victim. If the sleuth has not, other people connected with the case may well do. It may be that they expect certain positive or negative attributes of a person in that position (see the *Dialogue* section for a breakdown of these).

This can be profitably used in a number of ways. Firstly, a misapprehension can be exploited as a red herring. Secondly, the sleuth overcoming the wrong impression, through evidence, thought or some other means, can lead us closer to an understanding of the crime.

The Anti-Hero

Jimmy was the kind of guy who roots for the bad guys in the movies ... 'Goodfellas'

Basically ...

There really aren't any good guys in *Goodfellas*. Nicholson's man in *Chinatown* is a slimy piece of work. Dirty Harry is a thug. Most people in *Sin City* could spend a hundred years in jail without any injustice. The majority of people in Tarantino's world are cold blooded killers. All of the *The Wild Bunch* are ... well, work it out.

But aren't they great to watch?

Type Of Person

One of Bond's finest screen moments is when Sean Connery kills an unarmed man, then cheekily shoots his fallen figure in the arse as well, just for good measure. Some people worried this took Bond close to being an anti-hero, and it was a long time before this cold blooded element fully returned. Personally, Bond has never had more sly appeal.

That's the anti-hero in a nutshell, somebody who does what we probably won't, but will look damn good doing it. To the extent that we will want to be like them, somewhere inside.

Motivation

Well, what does an anti-hero do? They must show something we can relate to, probably a stronger presence in them than in us. Think in terms of cool defiance that can head towards evil. The anti-hero must be an exaggeration of one side of us. Take your dishonest or cruel side and really indulge it (in the story!).

Have you always wondered what it's like to receive a huge payment in a briefcase in a deserted car park? Anti-heroes do that. They also wear clothes we couldn't get away with, commit crimes we wouldn't and have a general cheek most real people can't touch.

Manners And Characteristics

A swagger is helpful, but some kind of strong taste is all you need. A bland anti-hero won't get anywhere. Remember, the anti-hero needs to do something to extremes.

Many anti-heroes, like the principles in a tragedy, have some flaw which is exaggerated or exploited to the point of ruin. Any of the seven deadly sins in some form usually fits well here.

Characters

If you have a strong enough character, or actor, an anti-hero can be whipped up out of thin air, simply through charisma.

Eccentricities

This can be anything that underlines the character's attitude. If they eat jelly babies with the right type of swagger, it works. The anti-hero has plenty of style, and whatever that style is, it must be honed and personal. These are, after all, people who live outside of regular rules, so their mannerisms will reflect that.

Bogart was basically an anti-hero in most of his roles, largely through being able to smoke in such a fashion with a face like that. His general manner is that of a charming scumbag, and we like watching those. Even when he was being noble the guy looked as though he was guilty of something. 'Nuff said.

Here's a quick checklist of what an anti-hero needs:

- Sleaze (essential)
- Charm (debatable)
- Defiance (useful)
- Excess (likely)
- Redemption (personal choice)

An anti-hero often tells society where to get off. The central character in Terry Southern's novel *The Magic Christian* (not a thriller but a superb book, strongly recommended) is an eccentric billionaire, Guy Grand, who's biggest pleasure in life is paying people to degrade themselves. He twists all manner of social norms – unleashing a panther at a dog show, coating money in sewage, hiring sky writers to tell all New York where to go – but often has a point to make. Sometimes he doesn't, though, and it's just fun.

I think that's fantastic.

The Two Kinds Of Anti-Heroes

There's likeable anti-heroes and unlikeable anti-heroes. The first kind have a touch of the scallywag about them, they're a bit sly and somewhat questionable. This type can have plenty of charm, like Henry Hill (Liotta in *Goodfellas*). They also often have a lot of admirable qualities, although honesty and trustworthiness are probably not among them. A degree of moral flexibility is a must.

It could be said that the division is, do we consider them acceptable as people for all their flaws? It's a personal matter.

Tony Soprano is a great example of the likeable anti-hero. Hardly a nice guy, he's still a decent enough feller in many ways. That his often playful, occasionally honourable behaviour masks a truly vicious, cruel man makes him the compelling character he is.

One of the main strengths of *The Sopranos* is its balance. There's whiny kid problems mixed in with mob wars, marital difficulties, friends' crises – Tony never gets it good for long. He's also got some psychological problems and a monster inside him of gargantuum proportions. At the height of his rage, Tony is so intimidating that going up to an angry Rottweiler and tweaking its nose seems far safer than crossing him.

The Sopranos uses mundanity superbly, and the family bickering and snide remarks about breakfast cereal allow for plenty of contrast with the rest of the drama. It's also a great way to show inside the various characters. From one character's good treatment of his wife it shows he is a far better man than Tony, for example.

Anything in this direction could well be headed for greatness, although I doubt James Gandolfini comes cheap.

More commonly, the anti-hero is just a form of likeable bad guy.

Steven Berkoff's hammy turn in *Beverly Hills Cop* is very entertaining, but not a patch on Alan Rickman in *Die Hard*. Both are ruthless, vile killers, yet Berkoff is repellent and Rickman is delightfully repellent. Probably he's just better at making evil charming, who knows, but there's an interesting division in reaction to these two characters.

While these two are both villains, Rickman is closer to being an anti-hero because he's so damn cool.

Similarly, two Pacino turns – definite anti-heroes, these – walk a line between likeable and unlikeable –

Tony Montana and Michael Corleone. For all Montana's swagger he's a deeply unpleasant character, yet we like him. Michael Corleone is a different kettle of fish; he develops into a cold, strong and utterly ruthless man. By the end of *The Godfather Part II* he's become such a hateful figure that the young man at the start of the first installment is unrecognisable by comparison.

How we react to such characters is of course personal, but there are some basic elements to be seen here. Somebody who is impulsive and bad with it is more acceptable than cold and bad. Loyalty is a fine quality, but we can relate to shrewd sense as well. The survival instinct can certainly be portrayed as admirable.

So, to test your own assessment, consider Mr White, Mr Pink and Mr Blonde. Which type of anti-hero are each of these? Consider the reasons why you think this. Does Mr Blonde being a psycho make him automatically unlikeable? How far does Michael Madsen's panache make this character's slightly anti-social tendencies acceptable?

Thinking about such matters (and they can be applied to a wide number of movies and books) will tell you something about your own judgements. These are made so instinctively we often aren't aware of why, but consider your reactions and the reasons behind them. If you want to create a good anti-hero, take this approach to your own characters.

Red Herring

Basically ...

A red herring is a false clue taking us in the wrong direction. A successful red herring is where we don't notice being diverted.

The phrase, incidentally, comes from days when young hunting dogs would be trained to follow a trail through the fish's powerful scent. After they had got used to this, the red herring was used to lure them away from the smell they should be following, thus the term.

Quite a lot of red herrings are done very badly. We have ready expectations of someone who looks suspicious, expresses delight the victim is dead, appears to be deliberately pinning blame on someone else and so forth. It is making these run contrary to our reactions that makes them useful.

Type Of Person

This elusive subject is a very useful addition to your storytelling, if any element of whodunnit – or whomightdoit, in the case of a crime yet to happen – is part of your thriller.

There are two types of red herring character – the ones who didn't do it and the ones who did.

The Ones Who Didn't

Some red herrings seem to be doing everything possible to attract suspicion. These can be used to your advantage in two ways, because either they really are red herrings (and haven't done anything) or they have and are behaving in a different way to what might be expected.

Peter Lorre, who played the child murderer in *M*, is often used as a red herring in old thrillers. The guy looks so suspicious, those wide staring eyes, the nervous manner and the high imploring voice. If you want to make a red herring character look as shady as possible, try watching a few Peter Lorre movies and seeing what characteristics you can adapt.

In the movie *What Lies Beneath*, when Michelle Pfeiffer's character is convinced a woman's ghost is haunting her, she believes her next door neighbour killed his wife. Several spooky setpieces lend credence to this, when the woman returns home from a holiday – clearly alive.

In *Donnie Darko* there is a man who appears periodically, dressed in red. He ... doesn't do a damn thing. A little joke on the part of the filmmakers, I think.

Characters can draw this type of attention to themselves by doing or saying suspicious things. Lying can make someone look guilty, as can expressing inappropriate sentiments (try to be subtle here – your red herring character leaping up and down shouting "I'm glad they're dead!

Whoopee!" when police question them is not very discreet) or being caught doing suspicious things.

Here the red herring diverts the audience so that some plot devices can go unnoticed. Similarly, having a cop suspect the wrong person, investigate them and find some suspicious details can lead us away from the right conclusion. It's like the young hunting dog being trained – a powerful lure leads us away from the correct trail.

The Ones Who Did

For this type of red herring to work, the character must be someone we don't suspect. There can be a number of reasons for this – perhaps they appear to be infirm, or of unimpeachable character, or in a position of trust that means we don't suspect them.

Spoiler Warning

The Usual Suspects has quite a few gigantic red herrings, misleading the audience and distracting attention away from the master criminal at the centre of the plot. Such a story is a considerable feat of writing, involving a narrator we trust when, of course, we shouldn't.

The fact that we go along with Verbal Kint's account of things as far as we do is a considerable tribute to the excellent script and flawless acting and direction. Of course, we have Verbal's pathetic plea that he was scared, manipulated, that he was covering up for someone else, and that magnificently delivered line: "What if you shoot the devil in the back? What if you miss?" as he holds up his withered hand.

Unsurprisingly, we cross him off our list of suspects. After all, the hypertalkative, rather pathetic figure is nobody's idea of a major criminal. This is exactly why the ending is such a revelation.

From this we can see that for this type of red herring to work, suspicion must be deflected. This can be done by having the guilty party hardly appear in the frame, or as someone who has been written off by the audience – perhaps because we've assumed they couldn't have done it.

Agatha Christie's *Death On The Nile* has a pair of murderers who are unsuspected throughout. We've been led to believe that neither could have committed the crimes in question, due to injury. The truth behind the injuries – precisely when they were received – alters everything, and means that people the audience had written off as immobile were actually up and killing, which is naughty of them.

This deflected suspicion is a prize example of how to make this type of red herring work. A trustworthy looking detective being the killer, for example. Again, *The Killer Inside Me* does this superbly. A lawman isn't exactly likely to be doing this, especially when he's the narrator. It works perfectly and is a breathtaking piece of work.

The Other Type Of Red Herring

Events can be a red herring, also. In *Fight Club*, Tyler Durden having an affair with Marla Singer – while the narrator observes – is a red herring, as it distracts us from the possibility that Tyler and the narrator are the same person. While we're looking away, the story continues and drives us closer to the revelation our attention has been distracted from.

In *The Long Good Friday*, a red herring occurs right at the end. (Spoiler warning) Bob Hoskins, having apparently dealt with his IRA problem, ridicules the mafia representatives who are leaving. (He delivers one of my favourite movie lines here: "The mafia? I've shit 'em!") He exits the hotel in a triumphant mood and gets in the back of his limo ... only to be faced by his about to be executioners.

In short, an incident that appears to be highly relevant, even definitive, to the story and is then seen as a distraction is a red herring. If we're being deliberately pointed away from something, it's a red herring. Basically, placing some unexpected situation or character before the audience as a diversion is the way to proceed.

Notice how this chapter doesn't break down the same way as the others on character? Ahhh, you were mislead ... exactly the point.

The Enabler

Basically ...

The enabler enables! He or she does exactly what it says on the tin. Whether your lead is a cop who needs a favour from Internal Affairs, or a soldier who needs help from top brass, or a family member who needs grandma to mind the fort while going on a daring mission, the enabler Makes Things Happen. And this covers wherever your ideas may lead you.

This may sound a little trite, so to put it in better terms – where have you seen the enabler?

Ben Kenobi training young Luke. M (and Q) in the James Bond films. Robin Williams in *Good Will Hunting*. The grizzled trainer putting Rocky through his paces. The shifty dealer selling Travis Bickle guns. Paulie in *Goodfellas*. The tolerant senior police officer covering up the upstart's "unorthodox" approach, such as Ronny Cox in *Beverly Hills Cop*. The bald guy Maverick keeps flying past in *Top Gun*. Doc Brown helping Michael J Fox get laid (and born – long story) in *Back To The Future*.

Type Of Person

The enabler is usually in some form of authority. He or she may be on bad terms with the lead, either temporarily or as a matter of form. This figure may be a guru, a watcher, a protector, an observer, a reluctant trainer (Clint Eastwood in *Million Dollar Baby*) and as the examples listed might show, the enabler can take a huge variety of forms and of course, their role is as big or small as you decide.

Motivation

It's generally to ensure that something prevails, whether it's justice or the path of a younger person. The enabler will traditionally be older than the character they're helping, and they've probably seen it all and been there and done that.

With today's increasing reliance on technology, the enabler may well be some techno-whizz, like Lucius Fox (Morgan Freeman) in the new Batman films. Of course, a lot of computer wizards are very young, so you may want to bear that in mind.

Manners And Characteristics

The enabler should have authority, either through age, rank, ability, disposition, experience or whatever else. It is a good idea to make the enabler reluctant, as this adds to the tension (will the central character get fired even if the killer is brought in? Pah! Those assholes at City Hall can eat my badge). Also, we wonder if our hero will get the assistance needed, as when Rip Torn shows up in *Dodgeball* (extreme example, as spanner throwing isn't always required).

Eccentricities

The enabler is often a curmudgeon. Often they will be helping someone unworthy, who's younger than themselves (and in the Hollywood versions, a lot better looking) and has the world at, or near, their feet. No wonder they can seem a bit sour. But that's just one convention.

3
Showing and Shaping Characters

Showing Character

Give Us Something Telling, And Soon

Quickly delivering a sense of what a person is about, or a piece of work, is a big part of establishing character. We need to see something that reveals them. A telling detail, an unusual reaction, can show us a very great deal. Several well placed scenes, hopefully naturally delivered, and we start considering their personality in our mind's eye.

We're Talking About The Build Up

With the exception of pastiche characters – such as quick light relief in whacky next door neighbour form – to show a character properly takes some time. We need to see how they react to situations, and what their own approach to life is.

It May As Well Be Right From The Start

Se7en is a briliant piece of film making. Right at the start – the first shots, in fact – we see Morgan Freeman dressing for work. He's dressing in such smart clothing that we wouldn't think he's a cop. He puts a fountain pen in his pocket, then collects a flick knife and a gun. He has a grim expression on his face, clearly one doing a duty. The grey ambience and the rain also set a grim tone. Then we cut to a grotesque crime scene.

Detail Is The Key

The smart clothing and fountain pen say a lot about Somerset's character, as does the whole scene. The film has also been very strongly introduced, the dour mood presented in no uncertain terms.

After the crime scene and a brief chat with his replacement, Brad Pitt's Detective Mills, Somerset is shown trying hard to sleep amid rowing neighbours, his steadily ticking metronome as an aid to calm. The jangling title sequence follows, where jarringly placed credits intersperse with footage of the killer attending parts of his business, although that only stands out later.

Telling Us What We Need To Know ... Fast

In these first five minutes we have a sizeable amount about the movie, its protagonists, and tone. The emotion is superbly controlled, with unpleasant and forboding images shown in half light around the edgy, mistrusting dialogue of the two detectives. Before the story has progressed very far we have a firm grasp on the characters and the type of material.

The Story's Progression Develops Each Character

A further sense of dark enters when Somerset asks to be reassigned – he realises after only the first body that this is part of a series. Clearly he's very smart, and more objective than proud. Mills we can see isn't stupid or naïve, but he has a sense of commitment that Somerset's cop no longer has.

Show Don't Tell ... Or Let Things Emerge Naturally

There's umpteen ways of showing character, but it needs to look natural. Beneath are some suggestions and opinions. As ever, go with what works for you.

Everyday Life

Showing part of a routine is good, as we see how the person behaves ordinarily, probably in their regular environment. How that character differs when under stress or in an exceptional situation is going to alter the way we understand them. The routine works as both an introduction to a character and as a contrast for later.

When we see a character going about their regular business, not only do we see them, we also see how other people regard them. Are they well respected, looked down upon, popular, isolated, hard working, lazy, ambitious, just treading water, do they have kids, are they their own kids, is their partner happy with them?

All these things can speak volumes about a character and allow you to show the audience who your character is quickly and effectively.

A Stressful / Threatening Situation

It's been said that in times of stress and threat we find out who we are. When confronted with danger we get the adrenaline of fight and flight, that can lead up to unprecedented speed, strength or aggression. There's also the question of what's important to us, like who or what would you save first from a house fire?

In one of his autobiographies, no less a legend than Johnny Cash talked of an armed robbery at his family home. A robber threatened his son at gunpoint. Cash mentioned how helpless he felt, how he would have done anything, sooner than see his son die.

Positions like this bring a lot to the surface – the values and emotions are really an acid test of who we are. When characters are in danger, whether they are noble or pathetic, this should be borne in mind.

Temptation / Corruption

No such thing as a free lunch? Any quick or easy step usually has a pay off attached. Employees being tempted to fiddle the till. A scheming lover may use influence to encourage some theft or abuse of position. A normally honest cop in financial trouble takes a bribe they'd usually refuse. The victim of a robbery deciding to fiddle the insurance.

Characters Being Lead Astray

When people are taken outside of their regular experience, we see different sides of them. This might be excitement, fear, revulsion (at themselves or the situation) or a whole host of other attributes we haven't seen yet.

All of a person's normal behaviour alters when they take a step like this. They are out of their comfort zone and regularly established behaviour. All manner of extremity of reaction can occur. The culprit may well blame old problems, previous mistakes, or cite some virtue ("I was the only one not on the take") as justification.

Loss

Bereavement effects people differently. When we lose someone close, our behaviour can show a variety of things. It can also give some clue as to the history between the two people, and that may be very useful as to what is going on.

If you have a character, especially a sleuth, lose a friend or partner, please don't go for the clichéd anger / revenge option. This could make sense, but a more studied response is likely to impress the audience more.

If you lose someone close, is anger the uppermost reaction? Unlikely, even if there are elements you could well be furious about. Loss, at the end of the day, is about grief, sorrow that the deceased is no longer part of our world. Anger may well come later, but the strong sense of bereavement will most likely be the initial response.

It All Leads To A Bigger Picture

Any of these things, or a variety of similar situations, can present the audience with various sides of the character.

As with the example of *Se7en* at the start of this chapter, look for ways of showing character that are quick and definitive. Not every cop wears a smart suit and carries a fountain pen. Similarly, you can find refuse collectors who make a point of dressing sharply outside of work, or fashion models whose hobby is gardening.

People Come In All Different Forms

Individuals are very different and a new perspective is refreshing. If your character has one or two seemingly definitive characteristics, look for a detail outside of this area to tell the audience some more about them. Remember, the more interesting the character, the more interesting the story.

Making the Goodie Really Good, Or Why Not An Anti-Hero?

How Virtuous Do We Expect People To Be?

Does a 'goodie' really have to be good? No. And how good is good anyway? Some heroes are so sickly in their correctness you just want them to get caught with a stolen hoard of cocaine and dead mob witnesses.

This is Cliff Richard / Donny Osmond Syndrome – whiter than white, and really annoying. One thing I love about James Ellroy is that even the good guys are dirty enough to warrant major prosecution, and this makes them compelling. Mr Boy Scout, the boring, anal, by the rules bastard, needs shooting or dirtying up. A squeaky clean good guy who gets dirtier in is an interesting figure – bear that in mind.

People Are Admired For Their Strengths ... And Loved For Their Weaknesses

Everyone loves an anti-hero, when they're done well. If that's too much for you, remember that basically, we have to like the sleuth, or relate to them, or just find them interesting. People with some grubby tones are usually far easier to accept, I suppose because they seem human. Also, nobody likes the moralistic Mr Clean, unless they suffer a horrendous fall from grace, which can be great entertainment.

Incidentally, if it seems dumb to call characters 'goodie' and 'baddie,' we all simplify to some degree, so I'm using this as shorthand.

Is Regular Life Too Bland For A Thriller?

Alfred Hitchcock said that drama was life with the dull bits left out.

In ordinary life people do good things, but these can be drab. Taking out the rubbish or collecting the kids is all very good, but people don't want to watch or read about it. Right?

Is Real Life That Dramatic?

Again, depends how it's done. Margie in *Fargo* (Frances MacDormand's Oscar winning turn as a pregnant police chief up to her neck in murder and, ooo, it's a great film, watch it) has morning sickness, an artist husband who wants his painting on a stamp, a lecherous nutty old school friend, an obviously lying man with a kidnapped wife, three dead bodies … doesn't seem so everyday and dull when it gets added up.

She's presented as very commonplace, and that's one reason why the film works so well – Margie's so unflappable and capable. We, the reacting audience, can hardly believe it and consider her life mundane. By comparison with what she deals with, it is (and so is ours).

Characters Can Be Build By Community

A rather touching performance from Sylvester Stallone can be found in the underrated *Cop Land*, an intriguing premise about a community outside New York where, uh, cops live. Stallone is the sheriff who missed the big time and is surrounded by big shots.

As he's starring with Keitel, De Niro, Ray Liotta and Robert Patrick (the T1000 in T2 and Johnny Cash's dad in *Walk The Line*), there is a measure of irony here. Amazingly enough, Stallone fills the screen with good acting, fully realising the character's disappointment. He is, basically, an ordinary man, rather run down, who gets pushed around a lot, and his mundanity – no slow motion sweaty punches or exploding arrows here – makes him real. If Stallone can pull this off, you can.

Making the Baddie Really Bad – and Original

"It is far safer to be feared than loved" - Machiavelli

Evil is entertaining. It's a riot. Famously, in *Paradise Lost* Satan is the only one who has any fun. That isn't saying much. Milton wasn't exactly a barrel of laughs and epic poetry isn't really entertainment. Out of the whole Eden, heaven and hell kaboodle, Satan rocks. God is pompous. Adam is wet, Eve sulky, and the angels suck. Milton shot himself in the foot.

Part Of Us Wants To Be Like That

We can't help admiring the cool of Verbal Kint as he walks out of the police station. Seeing the expression on Tony Montana's face as he fills his pockets with bullets and grenades is an experience. Sharon Stone's turn in *Basic Instinct* (and say what you like, she's a creepy customer) titillates and challenges.

We like evil – it's fun and when done well, we get a thrill of having safely visited the edge. Just as a rollercoaster gives safe thrills, the Terminator blasting through a police station has us tensely breathless.

The Terminator was the 1980s, though, and surely so much else has been done to push the boundaries by now. In fact, by this point, one might say that every possible little trick has been tried, and that to attempt anything new is a pointless exercise.

I think this is nonsense. For one thing, many genres have been written off only to be completely redefined. Romance films had this issue until *When Harry Met Sally* broke new ground, and then again with *Pretty Woman*. The gangster movie had the same problem before *Goodfellas*, then *Reservoir Dogs*, and even before Hawks' original *Scarface* in the 1930s.

Nothing Is New – Except Different Takes

So please don't consider any type of story old hat. It's a cliché, but some people consider there are only seven plots (and also seven jokes, for some reason). This may be true if you boil away all other details, but to consider this a limitation is daft.

Revenge plots, for example, could have been considered old hat when the Ancient Romans took the reigns over from the Ancient Greeks. The only difference was, they didn't call themselves 'ancient,' and yet their staple plot is still being reinvented and made fresh today.

So ... What Haven't We Seen?

In the Coen Brothers' *No Country For Old Men*, Javier Bardem is dead eyed perfection as the evil lead. He leaves death everywhere, and for a variety of reasons: convenience, revenge, self defence and theft. Also pleasure. The lives of the innocent are decided on a coin toss.

There is the novelty element of this bad guy using a slaughterhouse tool to kill people. He also asks key, sinister questions while deciding to murder people. This, with amazing direction and a top quality performance, makes him eerie and nightmarish.

Superb.

Scorpio, the protagonist in *Dirty Harry*, is discussed elsewhere, because he too is an excellent example.

Make Evil Distinctive

By way of contrast, a bad example of this – in my humble opinion – is Bruce Willis' "Kansas City Shuffle" speech in *Lucky Number Slevin*. For what else works in this film (I'm a big fan of Bruce and consider he deserves to be a movie star), for me this doesn't. It seems empty and contrived – perhaps it's lazy writing, or just not handled properly.

I don't know – why not contrast *Lucky Number Slevin* with *No Country For Old Men* and see why this element works in one but not the other? Maybe you disagree. As to originality, a sinister nutter asking mad, scary questions of his prey could seem overdone, but in *No Country For Old Men* it works beautifully.

Find A New Way Of Making Things Work

As Hamlet said, "The tale is in the telling." *Hamlet* is, after all, a thriller. There is incest, murder, revenge, greed, corruption, just like *Chinatown*, only with more doublets. The elements are the same but done very differently – the exact point of the quote. Please remember this if what you are thinking of doing seems to "have been done before." Most things have, but in a different form – *Hamlet* and *Chinatown* are good examples of this.

Don't be lazy here. A good bad character is an essential part of a thriller. What makes someone creepy, scary, or just plain *wrong* is down to individual touches.

Evil Comes In Many Different Forms

On TV, one of Inspector Morse's best villains, played by a sinister Iain MacDairmid, is a civilised, urbane wine lover, who is very like Morse. However, he is capable of arranging murder with the same detachment of someone ordering coffee.

Is It Time For Dinner?

A mixture of the highbrow and the pscyhopathic brings us to Hannibal Lector.

This fantastic creation has a real bogey man quality. He has a brilliant mind, outrageous faculties and some tastes as barbaric as his others are refined. He has other worldly gifts – he smells sticking plaster and a specific brand of toiletries on Clarice Starling ... eww, creepy!

With his penchant for chewing flesh like a terrier and terrific intellectual feats, Lector has an animal / superman quality. He seems to be the best and worst in people, both incredibly cultured and prescient as well as terribly savage. He gets fan mail from other serial killers. How far off the scale is that?

When I was 17, *The Silence of the Lambs* movie came out. There were claims of how disturbing the film was – brilliant publicity that made millions flock to see it. I can still remember the anticipation. How bad could it be? Surely it would be a disappointment after such hype?

For all the tense moments elsewhere, it is Lector who captivates, particularly his escape. I was on the edge of my seat, teenage cool out of the window. The sequence ends with one of the best "He's behind you" moments I've ever seen. Yes, I'd say it delivered.

Be Careful Of What To Leave Out

Lector is a fine example of a villain. With sequels *Hannibal* and *Hannibal Rising* there is also a good example of how to spoil such a creation. By explaining the seeds of Lector's evil, and his more ridiculously cultured mannerisms (having a special device to pour wine is just plain silly if you want to be a respectable deviant, sorry), the spell is broken and his mystique gone, all through overindulgence.

By comparison, if *Dirty Harry* contained a scene where the young Scorpio is significantly traumatised, some of the enigma of evil (how does somebody get to be so unpleasant?) is lost. For me, this pulled Lector's teeth out; which is a damn waste of a fine psychopath.

Having said how to avoid spoiling such a good wicked creation (I apologise if this seems contradictory), let's consider Lector in detail.

The good: amazing mind, well travelled, well read, fantastic doctor and psychiatrist, great with words and drawing, wonderful memory, thinks of your feelings.

The bad: kills people, eats them, chews nurses, cooks bad musicians and feeds them to (unsuspecting) dinner guests, thinks of your feelings so he can get in your head and boogey about to his loony heart's delight.

What can we conclude from this? Be open minded when being fed unidentified meat. Also, that a mixture of the highbrow and the obscene makes a great combination for a villain.

The Silence of the Lambs made serial killer movies popular to the point of oversaturation. The success of the Lector books ensured we were soon bored silly with serial killer stories. Then – yet again, originality making the old new – the movie *Se7en* came out.

Anything Can Be Made New

Se7en had a lot to recommend it. Morgan Freeman and Brad Pitt both gave superb performances and their old cop / young cop unlikely pairing etc neatly avoided the 'buddy buddy' cliches. They argued and annoyed each other, but in ways that made sense for their characters. There in itself is one tired situation being made new and fresh.

The best thing about *Se7en* for me, however, is the way it turned around expectations of a serial killer movie. While his crimes dominate the film, we only see John Doe near the end, when he walks in to a police station and gives his blood spattered self up. That is original in itself, and of course he has his own inspired reasons for this.

He, like Lector, is cruel, murderous, erudite and mad. It is a tribute to Andrew Kevin Walker's excellent writing that none of this appears to be trite or derivative, and it isn't. Even the killer's religious fixations have a sufficiently grotesque nature to avoid seeming dated. This is largely due to the extreme way this is expressed and the maniac levels John Doe will stoop to. He is an insane zealot and, in short, nightmarish.

The crimes are based on the seven deadly sins. Thousands of writers, kicking themselves for not thinking of this, must have been committing the sin of envy as they watched. I was. The murders themselves are gruesome, obscenely original acts. They are superbly revealed. The series of polaroids detailing the way the paedophile decays is a masterclass in storytelling, fast exposition that revolts and intrigues.

Preparing our emotions for the finale, Morgan Freeman tells his younger partner not to be surprised if John Doe turns out to be the devil himself, or if his head opens up and an alien flies out. Doubtless many people in the audience found their own tension both relieved and heightened by this bold, inspired speech. It's a terrific touch.

Se7en invites us to guess what happens next, both to prepare ourselves for the horrible crimes and also to feel smarter than the killer and the writer. It is an excellent example of making clichés new.

In short, however the baddie is made bad, do it well. Clichéd situations only stink if they're being done in a clichéd way.

Dialogue and Language

Talk The Talk

This is extremely important. The wrong phrasing can make your dramatic moment ridiculous, your hideous badass suddenly as scary as ice cream, or leave your bold intelligent hero looking like a flatulent berk. So Be Very Careful Here.

Make The Words Fit The Character

As an illustration, one very badly dubbed movie (and movies should always have subtitles, to avoid the following mistake) was an early release of *The Killer*. Chow Yun Fat's OTT assassin was dubbed with a very posh English voice. This hard as nails killer was left sounding like a wally, saying things like "I say, give me the money old bean, or I'll shoot you in the bally face" and frankly it was just plain wrong.

So, who is the character you're writing about? Most likely there will be several to consider in any particular scene. Knowing something about these people beyond their obvious contribution to the plot's development will make them more believable.

There are some issues to consider first of all. These can be a key to how someone talks. Using any of these as an entry point to develop your impression of how someone should sound is an excellent start.

Place

Where are your characters from? If they're from LA, they should sound like it. If you haven't been to LA, either go or pay attention to whatever you can from the area. Or, just go with the language you feel suits best. If you have nothing authentic to offer, either do some research (preferable) or go with your gut. People are people the world over, after all.

If you haven't spent long in a place, tailor your own language around the type of people you write about, judging by who they are.

Job

Jobs can define the way people talk and react. Certain pieces of slang go along with various professions, as do certain attitudes. Ambulance staff see accidents in a different way to police, for example, just as lawyers view clients differently to accountants.

If a criminal is high up the food chain, the conversation will run differently from a low level dealer. Are they part of a gang or other organisation, or more the lone wolf?

We expect certain things from people according to their job. We expect a teacher to be well spoken, whereas a mechanic with the same type of speech would seem exceptional. For small characters this is fine, but for big characters ask, who is this person? How do they talk?

If somebody has been doing the same job for decades, they are most likely stuck in a rut, or at least a routine, and the way they talk and conduct themselves will reflect this. Similarly, a habitually unemployed person has a different aspect to somebody who runs their own business.

Remember who your characters are, and that some things that will seem exceptional for their status will not strike the audience as convincing. Try to make it all add up.

Position In Life

A homemaker will often be both harrassed and capable. Someone without children has more time for themselves and their interests. A judge talks differently than a road sweeper (probably). We expect characters to reflect who they are in life, so consider accordingly.

The way people live influences how they talk. Someone living in a house share with four 20 year olds will sound different from a person who lives with their parents, just as a lonely divorcee will talk differently from someone who lives with hyperactive teenagers. Bear all these things in mind, and if you don't know the answers, ask yourself what's reasonable and make them up! This is a creative activity, after all.

Interests

Does a gun enthusiast talk differently from a guitar buff? I'd say so, just as an armchair sports fan varies from a keen competitor. If a character's interests are key to the plot – like bowling in *The Big Lebowski* – then establishing some teammates, some routine or other part of such life can prove useful to us in understanding these people and appreciating the way they talk to each other.

Remember that the interests of your characters can provide you with a good variety of opportunities. There are acquaintances from this field, special interests (such as competitions), equipment that can be used in crimes (a lot of sports gear could be used as a weapon) and of course team mates, betting, access to training grounds and so forth. Any of these can be profitably included.

Class

Someone who gets a six figure salary sounds different to those on a low wage, if only in terms of confidence. Upbringing, education, jobs, outlook, income – all these things are a part of class. People in a posh neighbourhood will naturally talk differently to those who live in slums.

Having a clear idea of where each of your characters is from will help you decide if the language you're using for them is appropriate. Their approaches to things also feature here, as some attitudes don't seem to fit various classes.

Monologues

When people are speaking to an audience (or themselves, but we overhear) they will talk differently than they will in conversation. If somebody is considering their life, a situation, some crisis facing them, then the way they speak is going to be direct, perhaps painful, and certainly different from their everyday conversation.

We expect people to sound very different when considering things privately. When someone takes stock, of a situation or their life in general, we expect a certain amount of soul searching. How do you sound to yourself when assessing big issues in your life, a relationship, say, or an upcoming crossroads?

Bear in mind that most of the above come with a wide variety of presumptions. Using a little imagination can take an expectation and turn it on its head, a useful way of making memorable dialogue.

Who's Speaking Now?

Consider each person you are writing dialogue for. Ask yourself some basic questions about who they are and how they fit into the situation.

From The Smallest ...

For the smaller characters, ask yourself how the main players will consider them. For these players, the plot device / help the scene along types, a few recognisable details are all we need. Are these people pleasant? Thoughtful? Trustworthy? Sociable? Suspicious? Greedy? A little while spent considering these can reap dividends.

... To The Most Important

When it comes to the main protagonists, think carefully how each fits into the appropriate category. Making a list, either mentally or on paper, will help you realise the things you are clear on. More importantly, it will show the things the audience may need clarifying.

What Type of Language?

Is Offical-Speak Ever Rude?

Years ago I had to give a police statement after seeing an assault. After delivering my account, complete with a fair amount of (verbatim) cursing, I asked if the swearing would get read out in court. The man taking the statement told me yes. Juries hear far worse than a few rude words, as do judges.

Keeping It Real, If Real Is What You Want

That policeman made a good point. When being arrested, a career criminal is unlikely to say "Confound you, infernal busybody!" although it might be rather entertaining if they did. However, I don't really want to spend time and effort campaigning for greater erudition among criminals, although having taught English to a mixed bag of teenagers, you could argue I already have.

Similarly, real people don't talk like Tarantino characters, which is something I used to regret at parents' evening. The dialogue works superbly in his movies, though.

It also begs the question that people could be convicted if the jury don't like their potty mouths. I wonder what it feels like to leave the dock, condemned, and having to suspect that.

First Of All, What Type Of Language Do You Use?

In stories, if rude words aren't you, I'd leave them alone. People who curse tend to do so naturally – through their mood, habit or situation. It depends on the impression you want to create. Naturally in some situations people curse – hit your thumb with a hammer and what do you say?

To contrast, look at Orson Welles in *The Third Man* or Cagney in *White Heat* – no profanity needs to pass their lips for us to be riveted, convinced by desperation and evil. So if you find certain words or phrases, unpalatable, it doesn't need to matter in the least.

Making Words Seem Natural

This Holy Grail of dialogue writing is a hard thing to accomplish. The conversations must seem natural for the characters, the situation and the place. Naturally, listening to people helps, whether it's in the bus queue, the bar, the workplace, or any place that you hear conversation.

Some people – and places – are synonymous with certain types of speaking. Laid back surferspeak, glib pub observations, laconic drawls – there's a wide variety of differing conversational styles. As with anything, it's what works for you and what you can make work.

How Do Your People Talk?

In Tarantino's world, what his characters say fits in completely, which is part of why his films work so well. The same can be seen in Kevin Smith films. While they aren't thrillers, the quality of the dialogue is superb and fits his characters and particular scenarios down to a tee.

In this area, in terms of an example, one name stands head and shoulders above the rest – Elmore Leonard. Read any of his books. That's how you do it.

Comic Relief

It's Letting Out A Bit Of Nervous Energy ...

Even around some really tense bits, we've all laughed surprisingly hard at some part of a movie. It's the situation the joke happens around that often makes it so funny. What could be mildly amusing becomes irresistably, uproariously amusing – if you've been tense.

The light relief is useful, as it can relax the audience before you hit them with the real dynamite. It adds to the overall enjoyability of your project. At the end of the day, the audience should be entertained.

Here are a few quick notes on how the light relief can be included.

The inept assistant is often grounds for a laugh. Imagine somebody in the wrong place, at the wrong time and perpetually doing the wrong thing. This can be a role for the sidekick or, in some cases, in addition to the sidekick.

As With All Humour, Timing Is The Key

Scenes of violence or high drama are often grounds for humour. The biggest laughs in most thrillers happen during, or after, scenes of high tension. *Hostel* has a scene where a sadist skids on a patch of blood and drops his chainsaw on his leg, which it proceeds to chew through. After such gut wrenching tension, it's a big relief.

We All Enjoy Some Attitude ...

A well placed piece of embarrassment can also do the trick. A character appearing to total disadvantage can be hilarious as, well, indignity makes for good humour. Some of Dirty Harry's put downs to his superiors rank here, not to mention Nicholson's priceless humiliation when he realises that a spectactularly unamused Faye Dunaway just overheard his crude joke. That's the mark to shoot for.

... And Some Fool Tripping Up

Slapstick can be good, but don't overdo it. And get it right – the recent slew of Hollywood 'whoops, I'll roll my eyes as I go head over heels' pratfalls are contemptibly bad. Avoid that.

Relationship Trouble

Everyone's A Little Bit Dysfunctional ...

A problem between two people who are in a close relationship can create difficulties like no other situation.

I'm sure you'll have noticed that when a couple are going through a breakup, nothing much else seems to register to them. Each side will be busy in some form of dealing with the matter. It may be in the form of expressing their view of the other, moving on, trying to come to terms with their own opinion, canvassing everyone else for their views, rebounding with someone else and so forth.

Boy Meets Nutter, Girl Meets Psycho

Naturally, this is used a lot in stories. A hidden surprise in a relationship can really add to the plot – one side will be double crossing the other, using them, cheating, planning to bump them off, blame them for their own dirty work or some similar development.

Clearly this can be used to add extra voltage to a thriller. Suddenly finding that someone apparently very reliable is actually following their own agenda can throw in real spice. Also, a sense of betrayal or vengefulness can act as powerful motivators. When people's love lives hit the skids they can be capable of all manner of deed.

It's Not All Hugs And Kisses

Relationships that cause trouble in thrillers certainly aren't restricted to those of a romantic kind. Difficulties of a professional nature are also likely to cause mishaps – and an entertaining arc to add. Umpteen cops and private eyes have awkward relations with their superiors or some mentor figure. A few twists of the screws here can give a story that bit more power or tension, as well as providing plot opportunities and chances for comic relief.

4
Approaches and Details

Atmosphere

Getting This Right Is Half The Battle

Let's face it, thrillers need atmosphere like a curry needs spices.

In the first few minutes of *The Long Goodbye*, we see a slow camera move in an apartment, a man asleep, a soft jazz track – we know where we are. From the way the guy wakes up, smokes, and makes food for his cat (which he seasons – who seasons cat food?) we get a strong sense of him.

This is pretty much the essence of what atmosphere is – getting a sense of who we're dealing with.

Get It Right From The Very Beginning

The start of the *LA Confidential* movie does this superbly, with gangsters, sleaze, cops, stars and Tinseltown, all paraded before our eyes to the accompaniment of Danny DeVito's breathless narration.

Kathryn Bigelow's excellent *Blue Steel* grabs the audience in the first seconds, with cries of 'No!' being heard over the credits. Sounds of a violent struggle accompany a view of a cop easing her way down a corridor.

It's A Good Idea To Introduce Themes With The Tone

After the scene finishes, the credits continue over extreme close ups of a revolver, in loving, lingering detail. That guns are essential to the plot is shown here, as is the villain's predeliction for drooling over them. Then we see Jamie Lee Curtis's rookie cop preparing for duty. The elements that appeal to the killer – her authority and femininity – are suggested here, in voyeuristically intense detail.

The prime example is *Taxi Driver*. The menace of the smoke, the rising and crashing score, the jagged neon taxi breaking out from the mist like a shark's fin – it all points at horrible things and more. This opening has been compared to an inferno. Certainly there are terrible things suggested in the introduction – the contents of Travis Bickle's mind, the city he lives in, even human nature itself – and it's a masterful piece of scene setting.

So, How To Create Atmosphere?

Atmosphere hints and threatens. It's what we know straight away when we see or hear certain things. It shouldn't be about seeing everything, even if the start is direct. Fritz Lang's 1953 *The Big Heat* has an attention grabbing shot of a revolver on a desk, followed by a shot. It then moves to the aftermath, and the rest starts to unfold.

This is one way of doing things – by going directly to one area of the story and taking it from there. In terms of giving the audience a jolt, and making an effective start, it's admirable.

Do You Start With All Guns Blazing?

This approach can work superbly, as it does in the example given, but it's unusual. A more regular way is to tease us along. Some enticing images, and music that suggests danger and intrigue, are more regular. In a novel, details of the dark are required. Any good noir story can be instructive in this, and it's surprising just how effective some of these can be.

Other Ways Of Getting The Ball Rolling

Describing a person, a place or a crime scene is a good start. Chandler's story *Wrong Pigeon* begins by telling us about a very sleazy customer, and Marlowe is watching him with his usual suspicion. Lawrence Block's *Out of the Window* tells us about the victim's life, in a way that clearly tells us it's now over. Then it moves on to the velocity of falling bodies – a fine way of sharpening the reader's appeitite.

It's a beautiful contrast. As we hear about this waitress, we also find out about the sleuth who's telling us, as his life is compared to hers in places. That start is so atmospheric we feel the oncoming lurch of finding out how she died. It's a piteous end to a short life, and the tone is brilliantly conveyed.

What Makes For Good Atmosphere?

Good atmosphere needs to suggest mystery and danger. Menace is the order of the day here. This can be achieved well by having everyday life interspersed with a sinister element. The narration of *Double Indemnity* does this wonderfully. This guy is just driving over to pick something up, and then we hear about the House of Death, and not only that, but the infamous House of Death it is presumed we have read about.

Wonderful. In terms of going from mundane to extraordinary, that succeeds magnificently. The chatty style makes it all the more threatening.

It Needs To Shake The Audience's Attention

All of the examples given have a jolting effect, as though someone driving a tiny engined runabout is suddenly behind the wheel of a racing car. To create a breathless sense of pace, a good start is essential. It's like getting off on the right note with someone – a bad first impression is hard to get over.

Make 'Em Flinch – Effectively Unpleasant Violence

Crossing A Line

The first time I saw the original *Assault On Precinct 13*, I remember thinking: There's no way that little girl's going to die, these films don't work like that. Wrong. I was shocked.

Making The Audience Cower

In the torture scene in *Gangster Number One*, we see it through the victim's eyes, as he lapses in and out of consciousness. Paul Bettany has stripped to his underpants so the blood doesn't get on his nice suit. He gets bloodier, more deranged; the room gets more dishevelled.

In *White Heat*, one of Cody's crew gets a faceful of boiling steam while robbing a train. I flinched – it's a horrible thought.

Giving A Sense Of Impact

What these things have in common is that they get in your head, in one form or another. The first is unexpected. The second is unusual. The third is just unpleasant – which they all are, of course, but the third one's in black and white, and shows no blood, unlike the others. So instead of graphic detail, we get graphic acting – the screaming, the sheer hideous discomfort. It's very unpleasant. Great job!

One Of Those Suspicious Distractions

The Dark Knight contains a fantastic scene that achieves this superbly. It's the second time we see Heath Ledger, when the Joker turns some goon's head into a pencil case.

The simple way he offers them a trick to excuse his interruption, while clearly unperturbed by all the gangsters, shows a viciously inspired, deathly cold mind. Obviously he's building up to something and audience anticipation rises.

When the payoff comes, it's shocking and fast, scarcely credible for a moment. We flinch and laugh at the same time. It's outrageous to the point where we grudgingly admire the sick bastard.

Keep Some Things Out Of Sight

The thought of violence can be just as effective as the spectacle, and more so. For all the blood in *Gangster Number One*, it's the wonder we have for the victim, what shape he's in, that powers the scene. The spectacle of his deranged torturer getting worked up, and messier, takes our imagination and dread to a higher level.

In *White Heat*, it's the sound of the wounded man's howls that makes us react. The thought of such injuries, such intense pain, makes us cringe. Not seeing the burns on his face raises our emotion and imagination.

As for *Assault On Precinct 13*, the unexpected victim – a little girl – gives the film so much more impact. It's vicious, it's well out there in terms of scope, in terms of what are we prepared to do. As it happens so quickly, and then moves on, we are momentarily stunned by the brutality.

In *The Dark Knight*, we see no blood. There's no after effect on screen – for the victim. We see the shock of the gangsters, even the admiring expression of one of them. This raises the level of proceedings – someone who can appreciate that, while only several feet away from it, is clearly well accomplished as a nasty piece of work.

Remember These Four Principles

To make a scene of violence effective, in one form or another it needs to meet one of these four criteria – shock at the victim, shock at the deed, shock at the effect on the victim and shock at the way it's done. There's umpteen ways of doing this, I've just picked four outstanding examples.

How To Make A Kill A Crowd Pleaser

Make Sure Someone Deserves It ...

The more despicable and unpleasant the criminal, the more we enjoy the death. Someone who crosses to really low territory, and who does genuinely despicable things, is naturally going to need a particularly satisfying end.

If the word 'criminal' seems misplaced, think of the Judas cops or lawyers who get it in the neck at the end of a thriller. We love their downfalls, especially if the way they die is served with some particular humiliation or gruesome twist.

... And That It Fits In With The Story

This needs to be balanced. There are umpteen second rate thrillers where the ante is upped right near the end, but done so in a clumsy way to make the villain's death more satisfying. Or, similarly, the cliché of someone falling off a building onto a spike. These have been ridiculously overdone, so try and avoid them.

Consider What The Audience Won't Expect

A surprising or inventive death can work wonders to give an end of piece kill more of an impact. Some supposedly passive or forgettable character popping up out of nowhere and shooting them can be far more enjoyable than seeing some burly cop put holes in their chest.

Similarly, a particularly unpleasant accident – falling into a cement mixer or being mauled apart by guard dogs – can achieve this just as well. In one Sherlock Holmes adaptation the killer gets his by ingesting an especially unpleasant poison – his own method of dispatching people.

That way, an extra dose of justice appears to be served, because the criminal's own device works against them. At the end of *Brighton Rock*, Pinkie's face recieves a dose of his own corrosive fluid – a suitably unpleasant end to such a character. What Bogart does at the end of *The Big Sleep* is another example of this working well.

Other Things Can Be Unexpected Too ...

The flipside of this coin is where the bad guy survives. This can seem a really cheap way of diddling the audience, but that depends how it's done. If there are two killers and one lives, that can leave a particularly unpleasant sting in the end of the tale. It can also add some satisfaction, if the one the audience likes more gets to live. Consider the end of

Approaches And Details

The Silence of the Lambs – we get extra shivers to know that Lector is out there.

Setpieces

In A Word ...

Heat. The gun battle in the middle can stand alongside the best and is one of the most compelling ever put on film.

Check The Build Up

As soon as the scene begins, there is a tangible feeling that prepares us. We see a business day, and De Niro's boys are clearly out for business. There is a tense low level percussion on the score and it sets an edge forward. Once the robbery is in progress the tense tapping beat is a countdown for the violence we know must be coming.

The scene is set over several very tense minutes before the first gunshot. As an audience, we are fired up for this. The cops start closing in just as the gang seem close to escaping.

Before everything erupts – and the scene has several primers – we are on the edge of our seats, waiting for the first move.

Once The Balloon Goes Up, Deliver!

When all hell breaks loose, as it massively does, the sound of the gunfire is huge. It is layered on the soundtrack to boom out overhead, the flat thunder of automatic weapons becoming incredibly menacing. Whether or not this is accurate I've no idea, but the effect is undeniable.

The camera switches between close ups and long shots, so that we alternate between the faces of those shooting and the distant view down the street, as if through the eyes of onlookers. The nightmarish destruction is brilliantly realised, and the exploding rage bursting out of the soundtrack strikes the viewer round the ears. Fantastic.

Don't Forget The Story!

The tension of the story is added to, as both the De Niro / Pacino protagonists lose a close ally, in Tom Sizemore and Ted Levine. While the film is undeniably slow in places, it is worth watching and rewatching for this one seminal setpiece.

The incredible photography, gunplay and soundtrack make this piece of cinema a stunning achievement. The timing of the violence, our familiarity with both the gang and the cops, the feeling of doom closing in – it's a masterful sequence. The rest of the film is one story angle colliding after another, but nothing else comes near this astonishing adrenaline rush.

What If You Can't Get What You Want?

A key 80's example was the fine piece of suspense and action towards the end of *The Untouchables*. Reputedly this was supposed to be on a giant set of a steam engine, but funding ran out so De Palma 'made do' with the main station in Chicago. However, it is brilliantly staged. The action is far slower than in *Heat*, and is largely slow motion. When it speeds up, however, the results are hugely effective.

In addition to the famous tribute to *Battleship Potempkin*, there is a cleverly constructed struggle between the key parts of the story. What is strongly conveyed is the strength of the Capone organisation against Ness' small band. The number of toughs and trigger men the underworld throw at this tiny, valiant group make for a gripping showdown.

There is an element of the gangster movie as an extension of the western here, with the sheriff staking his hand, and the remainder of his team (one), to bring things off. It isn't quite *Rio Bravo*, but there is some overlap in the themes. The heroics of a small, brave group against many hired thugs makes for a tense, exhilarating showdown, greatly added to by the odds.

A Less Well Known Example

Whilst these two examples are (justly) famous, some gems have been neglected by popular tastes.

French cinema is very underrated in terms of thrillers and noir, perhaps because some people find foreign language films automatically against their taste. As a general word, please try to get past this or you'll either miss some classics (across the board in foreign language films) or else sit through some truly dire dubbing. Avoid dubbing. If you bought a CD of opera classics, you wouldn't want some Karaoke artist singing the English version instead of Placido Domingo doing the Italian.

Plenty Of Bite

The *Dobermann* series of books have never been translated into English and I can't speak French, but the movie with Vincent Cassel in the lead, title role (a gangster of mythical proportion, cool and daring) is superb. The books, incidentally, are considered so outlandish that many producers thought adapting any of them was out of the question.

Going For Broke Across The Board!

Certainly the character is extreme, a hedonistic adrenaline junky who makes Vin Diesel's action man in *XXX* look like Grandpa Simpson. The energetic, rushing camera work reflects this perfectly, so does the movie's styling, which is urban noir on neon steroids.

The first setpiece is led into brilliantly. At a Christening ceremony, with the lead character in a pram, one of his hoodlum father's friends produces a characteristic present: a gigantic Magnum revolver. As he explains this, a Doberman Pinscher mauls his hand. The gun lands in the crib next to the baby, previously crying, now placid and happy, with this huge firearm lying next to him.

Not Letting The Audience Draw Breath

Cut straight to an armed robbery, with Vincent Cassel wielding the same gun at an armoured car, which he blows off the road. That's how the film starts, and it goes up from there. Slightly fantastical elements are brought in when Dobermann fires grenades from a little barrel under his pistol. As a mark of how good its styling is, what could be ridiculous is completely acceptable.

Dobermann is a classic modern noir. In addition to the slick, ruthless anti-hero, there's the hot chain smoking Monica Belluci. She's a hard-hitting customer and a wonderful way of presenting a modern femme fatale with extra badness – an excellent piece of casting.

In terms of bad guys, cue one extreme sadist played superbly by Tcheky Karyo (he plays the dodgy Russian general in *Goldeneye*). This guy is a seriously unpleasant piece of work, and the film works well as an example of what it takes for an anti-hero to come into his own.

Best of all, *Dobermann* is unrestrained. There are three superb lead performances, well supported by a group of freaks, extremists and nutters. The pseudo-religious killer, who puts a grenade in a policeman's helmet and sends him "to the heaven of headless men" is particularly wonderful.

And In Books ...

Did I hear anyone say books don't have setpieces? Rubbish.

Firstly, one of the finest pieces of detective fiction, complete with gigantic ending, car crashes, and quite extreme all round action is Ian Fleming's *Goldfinger*. Admittedly, this made a brilliant film, but reading the book gives you a very good idea of how such action can work on the page. Plus, the body count in Goldfinger's original plan was 60,000 – massively extreme and a detail which set the standard for future Bond movies.

Another superb book that made a fine film was *LA Confidential*. There are two main pieces in the novel that could be described as setpieces, the start (which was the basis for the ending of the movie) and an attempted prisoner break, taking place on a train. Just as some film directors' styles can make violence shocking and visceral, James Ellroy's prose is undeniably hard hitting. Every compliment he has ever received is justified by these two scenes alone.

Similarly, in his novel *American Tabloid* there is a fictionalised setting of the ill fated Bay of Pigs invasion. The writing has an epic feel to it, and the sense of grand horror is compelling and inescapable.

As with the setpiece in *Heat*, there is a mixture of the distant and the extremely close, as characters observe from a low flying seaplane, where the danger hits them even there.

Whilst some of the shootouts in the Mike Hammer books could qualify, I think the final scene to be mentioned here should be the blazing, astounding end of *The Killer Inside Me*. It's a mixture of action and plot revelation that ranks with anything mentioned here, and has the double impact of both intense, fierce action with a twist of giant proportions. A great ending to a particularly fine book.

The 'Pow' Factor

Just Giving It That Extra Wallop

There are several ways of giving a thriller that extra bit of power which makes all the difference. Sex and violence is obviously a fairly good starting point – that's a bit of a no brainer – but there are plenty of other areas in which some extra mileage can be achieved.

Many stories go from one way of pushing an audience's buttons to another. In one scene it might be fierce violence, in another particularly aggressive language, then unusual sexual behaviour and perhaps extreme attitudes to race, religion or gender. These are all things that can push the audience's buttons.

Making Things That Little Bit Better

A really successful story will have been considered from a wide variety of angles. Often this will be attention to small details – that extra bit of thought which can raise things to a higher level. All the small touches in *Pulp Fiction*, for example, mean that the film radiates quality because the details have been worked through so thoroughly. As a result, the film has no slack at all, despite having quite a few slow paced scenes.

So, How Can I Add A Little More?

Here's a quick checklist of what can be used to give a story that extra bit of a jolt:

- Any sexual twist or deviant behaviour
- Corruption where a prominent figure is shown to be a louse
- Especially good ways of killing people
- Particularly brutal or unpredictable violence
- Rare or powerful cars or guns
- A character with an unusual interest
- Aggression from an unexpected source
- Major level criminal conspiracy
- Huge amounts of money (there's something about lots of cash)
- Unusual places to leave bodies

Milk The Suspense

Getting Every Last Bit Of Tension ...

If that doesn't sound too classy, think of some fine stories where it appears that every single nerve has been expertly touched upon. There's nothing wrong with this, as it can raise the effectiveness to an entirely new level.

How Would An Expert Do This?

Let's consider a classic example of how this is done with *Rear Window*.

The suspicion (which becomes raging) starts off with a man looking furtive. He clearly doesn't want to be watched. Hmm. Okay. Then there's a dog digging in a flowerbed it left alone earlier. Next thing you know, the leads start discussing how you go about cutting up a body.

Where's This Leading?

The big question finally gets asked: Where is this guy's wife? Then other people start being won over to this line of thought and start going over what they know. The hunt for clues begins, and the possible gruesomeness of the crime is considered.

Include Several Different Views

With the police officer's arrival a more steady, rational voice is heard from, looking at the more plausible explanations. Has she gone on holiday? Have they had a row? Is a relative ill?

From this point, the plot thickens considerably as the curious dog turns up with a broken neck, and a master director takes it from there ...

Considering the deed from as many angles as possible brings out the most suspicion. Having details convincingly mentioned and questions explored makes the audience start to feel every last twist of the crime.

Rear Window is a fine example of this because it looks at the situation from so many different viewpoints. This way, the individual viewer's reaction is most likely covered by one of the opinions shown, and as a result the audience is likely to feel more involved. If our opinion is represented, naturally we feel more connected to the material; in this case the crime and its solution.

The Feel Of It

A High Standard Needs To Come Over

Anything that people really care about has a particular feel, an essential quality that nothing else seems to capture. This can be found in clothes, cars, houses, musical instruments, particular types of food and certainly applies to thillers.

This is hard to describe and for your own tastes, you will know this far better than anyone else. For anyone who has checked out a lot of movies, books, records (or anything else, for that matter) the notion of finding something that hits the same spot as another fine piece of work.

People Look For A Sense Of The Same Vibe

After the same spirit, many avid music fans will be checking out the back catalogues of music legends, trying to find songs that have a similar feel to some great song that really takes them somewhere.

Learn To Develop Your Own

One of the first major mistakes I made in writing was to try and repeat the atmosphere of a film I really liked. This was a huge error. If you are making a thriller at the moment, my advice would be to put other things as far out of your mind as possible and allow it to become whatever it is, just by itself.

It's very hard to let a project breath. You need to have a certain measure of confidence while getting away from the unnerving feeling of someone disapproving right over your shoulder. Forget that. Worry about that later (if at all). Just go with it and give it some elbow room.

Humour Potential

This Isn't Just For Spoofs ...

If you don't intend to crack a smile with your thriller, please don't skip this. Noticing how situations and characters can be used for comic effect can lead to an excellent understanding of how the story angles work.

Also – very important – it can lead to noticing that one wonderful aspect that really makes a story work.

Bear In Mind Thrillers Can Go Way Too Far

Anything that can be taken to silly extremes is prone to being mocked. Maybe it's deflating pomposity (such as this sentence) that makes people crack a smile, or the cliché done so far out of the window people can't help laughing.

Take The Expectations, Turn Them Round

The Naked Gun and *Dead Men Don't Wear Plaid* are both stunning examples of how funny it can be turning a thriller on its head. The poster for the latter always makes me smile (Steve Martin posing with a gun, and his shadow putting its fingers in its ears). The start of *The Naked Gun* is incredible. Please watch both.

Expectations

To make a spoof of something, expectations have to be there. My own publishing experience tells me that. When people think serious and get inane, well, don't call me Shirley.

Appearance

Silly outfits are most effective when kept to a minimum. Too many outrageous hairdos or priests in suspenders and the impact is lost.

Mentioning taste when covering a field that can cover so much squirting blood, tomato sauce or whatever may seem strange. Play the gags well is all I'd say, and too much of the same thing gets old very quickly.

Manner

Deadpan is the order of the day here. If anybody involved in this is aware it's supposed to be funny, I'd say you've had it. Think of the lamer spoofs where some gurning nitwit makes a song and dance out of a bad gag, so they've overexposed what was crappy in the first place.

The best thing that can be said here is, assume that none of the characters realise they're in a spoof. Having someone do something particularly inane, without realising in any way that it's supposed to be funny, is the best way to go.

Setpieces

If you plan to write a novel, remember books have setpieces. A lot of the funniest parts in Carl Hiasson or Kinky Friedman books are from classic thriller situations that have a special twist. Hiasson has his taste in sleazy grotesques, Friedman features cats, whiskey and a lesbian dance class. And I'm not saying either is wrong.

Setpieces will depend on the genre you are spoofing. Think of some classics in the field you're in (such as the court room scene in *A Few Good Men*) and ask yourself, what is the least likely thing to occur here? What would seem right out of place? What's the last thing you'd expect everybody to just ignore and roll with?

A few such questions and you'll have a pretty good picture of what you can do within the genre you're using.

Plot

A story can work with a minimum of this, provided it entertains. To be honest, I can't imagine anyone getting far trying to follow the plot of some spoofs, but by all means try. String a few situations together and see what suggests itself. This can certainly work elsewhere, so it may as well be used here.

If you're going for a traditional approach, such as a robbery, remember that the *Pink Panther* series of films worked very well with Clouseau as the sole source of amusement, at first. Later on, Herbert Lom's exceptionally well played Dreyfuss comes into the comic frame, but everybody else is deadly serious and only nonplussed at Clouseau's madcap antics.

Genre

The cop and whodunnit thriller have been very successfully spoofed. I think there's plenty of room to spoof heist and serial killer movies also. If you think of all that we expect, and then see how to turn that upside down, then I would say that was the best approach. Do remember that a good joke makes people forgive a lot, so if you feel you're being irreverent, that may be exactly what's required.

Angle

Often spoofs take a particular approach and do not vary it. So, for example, the angle may be slapstick humour or wordplay, or a straightforward reversal of expectations (such as an extremely well spoken street gangster). These can work fine, but why limit yourself? There have been a good many humorous thrillers that have varied their tactic, throwing in whatever gags they can.

When people talk of *The Naked Gun*, remember it really is a classic of its type. Some critics mention the high gag rate, that if one doesn't hit, another will soon enough. Given how many outstanding jokes there are, and the daft little pieces going on in the background, this covers so much ground. Here a lot is done very well, and what doesn't hit the mark doesn't matter.

Take A Stereotype, Use It Wisely

Frank Drebin, the Leslie Nielsen character, is perfect for ridiculous noir. So many genre expectations are milked – the ridiculous action scenes, the talks which advance the plot, the clueless sidekick, the clueless boss, lumbering investigative work being upset as Drebin turns many scenes into havoc filled silliness.

One of the best touches is the suspicious businessman with a diabolical scheme. The mayor is also involved, as is a police superior, a lab guy, the typical suspicious feller on the docks, the shoe shine monkey etc.

Some of the characters are as daft as Drebin, others played with admirable seriousness. Here we can see the beauty of a well balanced spoof – for all the visual jokes there are verbal gags that often require close attention. The 'nothing to see here' line, delivered with an exploding fireworks factory visible in the background, is a perfect joke.

What Can The Books Do?

Outside of movies, Janet Evanovich's Stephanie Plum novels have found a loyal readership. They concern a New Jersey native who's failed at a variety of jobs (including lingerie buyer – hey, no harm adding a little spice!) and desperation leads her to talk to a cousin and get the only job she can, that of bounty hunter.

It's worth mentioning here that this series has become extremely popular. Stephanie Plum has starred in 13 novels, I think, and I gather all of them contain similar ingredients. There is a wise talking, kick ass heroine and her coterie of family and weird friends, not to mention fresh baddies every book. The novels are funny and thrilling, a great combination if you want to move into this area. If this is your intention then you are well recommended to try these out.

Carl Hiasson has also made an excellent living out of keeping enough thriller elements in with the comedy. Again, people wanting to move into this area should read *Striptease* (although I can't recommend the movie). The jokes are made beautifully, and there are many comic situations (the stripper crazed corrupt senator bringing plenty) and the plot even manages to be thrilling. It's an excellent read with a great deal going on.

Approaches And Details

If This Is For You ...

The best approach here is to read and watch a variety of these stories and see which appeals to you. Ask yourself which elements of the genre you would most like to satirise. Where can you see yourself making jokes without sacrificing the integrity of the story? If you can be both amusing and tense, as Janet Evanovitch can, then you will do well.

Music That Thrills

You Hear Certain Songs And You Are There ...

Certain films have soundtracks that add hugely to the impact. It is difficult to imagine the same emotions accompanying movies like *Mean Streets* or *Pulp Fiction* without the great, well chosen songs.

The Sounds That Sum Up Certain Feelings

Any amount has been written about the effect of music on the mind and feelings. Think of the lyrically bittersweet elements brought out in films like *Blade Runner* or *LA Confidential* where a flourish in the score reminds us both of the human element and both films' noir foundations. This music tells us a lot about the films, the stories, the characters and their separate roots.

The beautiful, lyrical classical music that introduces *Raging Bull* (*Cavalleria Rusticana*) offsets the brutal content; countering harsh scenes of violence with gentle, floating themes. We see a boxer at the peak of his form, an athlete whose graceful movements could be considered beautiful, being framed in our minds by sounds of great splendour.

This provides us with a benchmark for later in the film, when La Motta or his opponents are receiving such gigantic beatings that surely their heads cannot take the pounding. In these places, instead of the gently magnificent classical music we have the frenzy of ringside noises – the competitive bloodlust of the crowds, the trainers' calls for this or that tactic, the referee's input and the commentators' excited banter. The contrast with the earlier sounds makes the spectacle even harsher in the viewer's mind, raising the expert scenes we see to new heights of effect.

The Music Should Frame The Action

Crucially, the music has to fit the scene. To stay with Scorsese for a moment, the soundtrack in *Goodfellas* serves as a particularly useful example. Because writer Nicholas Pileggi had access to a good deal of FBI recordings, covering more than a decade of surveillance, he could hear popular songs of the time. As the bugs would be in bars, clubs and cars, the various conversations were naturally soundtracked to what was being played on the radio and at social venues.

As such, the music used fits each scene perfectly. It also adds to the greater authenticity of the real figures being portrayed having listened to the songs the audience hears. *Sunshine Of Your Love*, for example, was re-released in the late 1970s just at the point it is used in the film, when it is used to underscore De Niro's realisation that many of his associates from a huge robbery "have to go."

Rewatch the film and look at his expression as the opening bars are played – it works perfectly.

Some Things Fit Exactly

If it's the right sound for a particularly important segment of the story, then the difference between an inspired choice and a stop gap solution is clearly evident. The enormous care that goes into picking songs or composers for films can have an immense effect on the overall impact.

Music Can Reflect And Suggest Themes

Bernard Herrmann contributed great scores to many Hitchcock films. His music is precisely considered and adds greatly to the emotions that swirl in the films. The booming, orchestral pieces and suggestive, at times sinister, instrumental figures emphasise the story arc, and remind the audience of the character's emotions.

The famous (even notorious) images of stairwells in *Vertigo* are represented by the repeated use of triplets in the soundtrack. The constant reworking of the musical figure at the start gives an impression of sea-sickness and swaying. As the credits unfold, the music accompanies many visual references to weaving spirals and disorientating circles. The audience starts to feel the dizziness that the film's impact relies on simply through the music.

Similarly, the famous slashing music in *Psycho* gives the film extra horror. The repeated, harsh violin notes give the viewer a physical sensation of the brutal violence of the murders. It adds an extra emotional dimension to Norman's acts of madness. We see the killings and feel the tension, but it is the music we feel in the pit of the stomach, and that adds an appreciable horror to the macabre deeds.

Music Builds And Lifts Our Moods

Just as Hitchcock was a master of understanding how to milk an audience's emotions and fuel their fears, Herrmann used orchestras to give each film's drama increased depth. He brought out so much extra with the music it is as though all the films he worked on had far greater foundation in the mind of the viewer. This is film music at its most masterful.

The last work he completed before his death was the soundtrack for *Taxi Driver*. This is surely one of the most brilliant examples of a film's score enhancing and offsetting the movie's content. Scorsese – hardly a slouch at picking the right people – made exactly the right choice in obtaining Herrman's services for this key picture. The music he produced is exactly right for this arch tale of alienation, and Scorsese dedicated this fine work to his memory, a fitting tribute to a master.

Use Reality

Everything That Comes Along ...

It's amazing the things people hear, especially about crime, law and order and so forth. A lot of this is anecdotal but interesting. Some of it is simply attention grabbing – presumably it's grabbed yours or that of whoever is telling you, and that's a good start.

Keep an ear open for such things, as many of us tend to do anyway (some of it's intriguing, right?). However, do remember that there is a place for such tidbits as well as just conversation. I expect a lot of what passes for fact in some crime stories began as something the author overheard in a shop or wherever.

Rumours Can Be Very Useful ...

Here's an example of what I mean. My sister knows someone who lives in the Bahamas. Apparently, few white people are stopped for speeding there (draw your own conclusions), but if you are, the regular procedure is to say something like:

"I'm sorry, officer. My fault entirely. I suppose the fine's $50? Could I give it to you? Saves on paperwork ..."

And so forth. However, in the Cayman Islands (my sister's husband works in finance) it's the opposite. One guy got six months' imprisonment for trying to bribe his way out of a ticket.

So Long As It Sounds Right

True? I can't verify it. But it does sound like good detail, and you can change the places to anywhere, provided it sounds convincing. Also, in the Bahamas there are places called Go Slow Corner, Dead Cat Alley and Dumping Ground Corner – all with legitimate street signs, too. Things like that are perfect to adapt.

Keep An Eye Out For The Right Thing

The best example of this is how *Chinatown* got its name.

Robert Towne, the screenwriter, was in an LA bar having a couple of quick ones when he got talking with an off duty cop. Complaining about his problems, the guy mentioned that Chinatown was cop slang for "so messed up you don't want to go there."

Why? Because any officer walking the beat in Chinatown gets called in to mediate lots of deep, bitter rows, often relating to old feuds. All the complainants talk across each other in excitable tones and bad English. Hence Chinatown meant, leave it well alone.

A lightbulb could be seen doing the old idea business above Towne's head. He'd been researching land corruption in California and wanted some threads to turn it into a story. As such he used this, not just for the title but to spin a story covering incest, murder, adultery and you name it. Areas your average person would leave well alone.

If making films is your game, the director Steven Soderbergh maintains that *Chinatown* is an excellent example of filmmaking at every level. I'm not a director and wouldn't pretend to be more than an avid consumer, but I recommend you read what he has to say if you have a yen to stand behind the camera.

Reading Reality

Assuming you don't happen to hear the perfect device in passing conversation (which is not something to be relied upon, but be open minded, like Robert Towne), true crime books can be fascinating and contain plenty of likely stories, details and so forth.

If you like thrillers, quite possibly you'll enjoy true crime books. If you haven't had a go, try them. If you haven't liked them so far, try a different type (and there are many). Some are trash, others exploitative, and some downright fairy stories. Be your own judge. After all, most likely you're looking for some of the real life stuff that can give a story credence and grab the audience's attention.

The Ingredients Of A Good Thriller

The Traces Of Real Life

Recently I read of an undercover drug agent, who had used many kilos of cocaine in a drug sting. As he was dealing with a high up player, it had to be convincing, so he persuaded his superiors to let him sign out however much it was of the drug.

The guy he was setting up looked at all this cocaine, a fortune's worth of the stuff. Without trying any, or opening a single packet, or even touching one, he began sweating all over at being, well, in its presence.

To me, that's an interesting detail and one that could work superbly in the right place. Most people don't have the opportunity to put such things to the test, and frankly it wouldn't have occurred to me. From such books you can grab some great insights.

Reality Made One Of The Best Ever Thrillers

Perhaps the best example of this is Nicholas Pileggi's book *Wiseguy*, filmed as *Goodfellas*. Much of what makes the film so impressive are the little touches; signs of a top director, certainly, and one who knew where to get the details.

Pileggi had access to FBI surveillance tapes. Many of the scenes in the film have period music in the background, songs that were in the charts at the time and played on the radio – in the wiseguys' clubs, in their cars and so forth. Songs that were playing in the background of the tapes, incidentally. As such, the overall feel is one of reality.

Detail is presented impeccably. When *Sunshine of Your Love* is played, Robert De Niro's character is deciding to murder his Lufthansa heist crew. The song was on re-release at the time (late 70s, about a decade after it first charted) and let's face it, it's a cool song. Watch the movie again and check De Niro's expression as the track starts.

Keep An Eye On The Small Things

Bizarre details are important too. You don't need to mention their source, or whether it reflects well on you or your project. It doesn't matter where it came from, but how you use it. Some writers and directors are criticised for plaigarism, and this is important – but at times allegations of this are irrelevant.

For example, I thought *Reservoir Dogs* was stunning, and I was aghast at allegations that it had copied from *City On Fire,* so I watched it. I considered *Reservoir Dogs* far better. Maybe I was biased, and perhaps it doesn't matter. It's still a great movie.

That's one form of influence, and not a bad one – to use, or borrow, is natural. Shakespeare did so constantly, without which he'd have written some sonnets and maybe two plays. That might've been a good thing, but it's too late now.

Dialogue Plays An Important Part

Conversation is very important in terms of reality. The exchanges should seem natural and unforced. They should also be entertaining, though. Many people won't care if some things are realistic, so long as they enjoy it.

In terms of accuracy, I've seen dialogue quoted in court hearings which didn't strike me as that realistic, as it seemed artificial when taken out of that situation. It's a question of what needs to be done to make things work in a story.

I saw legal documents on gang killings when working for a lawyer. Office work may suck but once in (I'd say) five years you get an interesting job. And I'd still say that anecdotal detail is more important, but food for thought is always important.

One exception to this – and of course there are substantial things to be found under any stone – is how a young gang member, fifteen and stupid, put a Mac 10 machine gun next to a man's head, pulled the trigger and "was surprised at the effect."

(The man's head disintegrated. Shouldn't be that surprising, really)

Would an audience believe that, though?

What Is Realistic?

Hyperviolence in cinema (a pretentious term, I know) is one such area. I've winced umpteen times while people were graphically blasted back and forth, blood everywhere. Is that really representative of the damage pistols do?

I was in France once and saw footage of a Rio cop (bizarre is it? True nonetheless) killing two suspects.

Essentially, two bank robbers had been described as two guys on motorbikes with pistols, which is a bit vague. An enterprising Brazilian cop flagged down two motorcyclists and shot them, presumably so he could knock off work early.

A French cameraman caught it on film. It was fast and nasty in a way that takes some believing, but still, there it was. In England, that wouldn't have been broadcast; such footage would be deemed far too unpleasant.

The "suspects" didn't fly about the place bleeding everywhere. They dropped as if poleaxed. From a distance of around fifteen feet little blood was visible.

Were these films untruthful, then? No. If it's felt, then it's true. That's debatable and completely personal, like saying *White Heat* is as graphic as *Pulp Fiction*. They both hit the mark, and that's good enough for me. If you want more, good for you, go for it.

Part Two – The Grimmer Things

People Say The Strangest Things

A good friend of mine suffers from a terrible curse. He wears horrible tasteless floppy hats, which look like a cross between Alanis Morissette and Tom Sawyer. I'd never mention it, though.

One evening, after some drinks, we got talking about movies. Being the debonair sort that I am, I mentioned a tasteless (but nevertheless hilarious) college prank.

While watching *The Silence of the Lambs* on video, a friend of mine flicked some yoghurt at his girlfriend as Jodie Foster is leaving the cells ... during a seminal moment, if you like.

Anyway, sophisticated amusement to one side, my hat loving friend started talking about the real Behavioural Science unit, and how (apparently) its profiles are accurate in only 25% of the solved cases. For the unsolved, I suppose it's irrelevant.

Everyone was surprised, but he does love true crime books so – and it's again with the details – maybe we shouldn't have been. What he said rang true, although I haven't sourced it.

Give It The Feel Of Being Real

It rang true much as the best fiction does. In other words, it was real, even if it was wrong – if that makes sense. It was a good foundation for a discussion, certainly, and that kind of mileage can go a long way in a story.

This was interesting, so I looked into it. It seems that some interested souls (clinical psychologists, tabloid writers etc) have narrowed some of the terms for various kinds of nasty down a bit. Someone like the Yorkshire Ripper, who targeted prostitutes, is not just a serial killer but a missionary serial killer. I thought this intriguing so decided to do some research.

Looking Into Some Darker Things ...

For anyone interested, there are five types of serial killer – visionary, missionary, hedonistic, comfort (killing for money, eg hitmen) and control. I'm sure there's plenty of story mileage in those.

According to the FBI, in the 1980s 35 serial killers were active. One expert claimed that 1990 saw 500 serial killers in the United States, each killing 10 per year. Between them this amounted for 25% of the country's murders. Whilst it's all very politically correct to regard the criminally insane as so productive, this seems high, but who knows.

The number of psychotic personalities on Wall Street, Capitol Hill and elsewhere is anyone's guess.

Making Use Of Such Information

Having one or two details or estimates up your sleeve can pay off. So can using them in conjunction with another premise – which I'm going to demonstrate now.

(spoiler – if you haven't read *I Am Legend*, skip a paragraph)

Richard Matheson's wonderful novel hinges around the creepy principal that there is one human being left and the rest of the world is populated by vampires. The novel has a chilling ending – the heroic survivor, the last man alive, is treated with revulsion by vampires. They see him the way we would view a vampire in a cage, as a freakshow to be feared.

This is a superb concept. To have such an idea in mind when writing a story must be awe inspiring, but such things can't be conjured out of thin air, right? Certainly. But what can we do?

Mixing Premises With Facts – Or Anything Else!

Let's combine this notion – essentially a role reversal – with some of the information from above and turn it around. Out of America's population there are only 500 who aren't serial killers. The rest are pack hunting animals who kill for whatever need; food, say, or pleasure. Or maybe it's just the done thing.

A typical day for them may go something like:

"Jim is an ugly sod. We should give him a five second head start then slaughter the bastard."

Jim would then get slaughtered, or someone else would by him, presumably. And so the long day wears on. Then we go to an FBI type organisation when they find the body of someone who hasn't been murdered and pull a no holds barred investigation until they find whoever didn't kill them … this wants some adjusting, naturally, but I swear there's a good idea waiting to get out.

Anyhow, you get the picture. Jumbling bits of things together, or turning them on their head – like that wonderful idea of vampire hoards regarding a regular man as a hideous freak – and you suddenly have some mileage, or at least the beginning of it.

Is Research A Platform Or A Millstone?

Some crime authors put tremendous stock in research. I have mixed feelings about this. Firstly, anything that works is terrific, irrespective of how true it is. This is fiction, after all. Secondly, the quality of some authors work seems to decline the more they research.

Some authors I can think of are sticklers for correct details. This is to their credit – to a point. With some I get the impression they have allowed detail to overcome suspenseful story telling.

This is a personal view, of course. However, knowing the precise location of the vending machines at FBI headquarters or the full details of a medical procedure are only important if the story is served well by them. At times the detail stagnates and the narrative flow is weakened by it. At the end of the day, a good story well told is the aim, not a lot of meticulous detail.

5
Last But Not Least ...

Don't Give Up!

This Can Be The Hardest Part Of All ...

Some things take a while to come into their own. Whether it's ideas sitting on a shelf, some old manuscript in a drawer or some piece of a story or character lodged in the brain, many great stories festered for a near eternity before working out.

It's the stuff of legend in Hollywood, how long some scripts take to come to the screen. *American Gangster* was almost filmed several times, with costs running into tens of millions in star cancellation fees alone. Similarly, every writer knows what it's like to look at blank pages and feel nothing coming out.

Quality Takes Time ...

Some things are worth waiting for. Would Sylvester Stallone have made a passable Axel Foley, Laurence Olivier a decent Don Corleone or Frank Sinatra an impressive Dirty Harry? These were the first casting choices, and it would seem an excellent thing they didn't happen.

So, if you find yourself coming up with ideas that seem bogus, or just don't fit, then leave it. That's not the same as abandoning an idea, just letting it come out in its own good time. Unless you want to

171

produce work that appears contrived or phony, that's the best thing you can do.

What To Do When Nothing's Happening?

When things aren't shaping up, don't worry. First of all, it's the easiest thing in the world to lose confidence. Bear in mind that some of the world's most established stories were all but disowned by their creators, and sometimes exactly that happened. The number of writers and directors who have fought bitterly is huge, with many having their names removed from incredibly well thought of titles.

Take A Broad, Flexible Viewpoint

There is no real solution to this, although taking a step back is a good idea. The main thing is not to quit if you believe in the project.

One of the best ideas is just to leave something for a while. It can be so much easier to come back to something with fresh eyes and a new approach. This prevents people from going down certain blind alleys and getting mired down in repetitive, self defeating lines of thought.

Last but not least, what follows is a list of great crime books and films. If you find your enthusiasm waning, or are in need of some inspiration, you could do far worse than check these out.

Recommended Crime Films

This could be a huge list, and is by no means definitive. What I would say is that each is a great example of a thriller. They all impresses and entertain, and if you've missed any, I'd recommend you check them out.

If any of my choices sound dull or uninviting, I would point out that some of these movies I didn't enjoy the first time round, due to the day I'd had or the mood I was in. If you haven't watched these movies, I would give them a chance. All are fine examples of how to get things right.

The Public Enemy – Cagney's first starring performance is a classic tale of street urchins progressing from simple mischief and thumbing their nose at the police to embracing organised crime. The first kill of a policeman, when a line is well and truly crossed, is when the developing criminals start to realise how little they can rely on people who aren't in their close circles, and start keeping heavier company.

As with many films of the period, it focuses on the family tragedy of a young man going bad. Not for the last time we see a remorseful Cagney surrounded by grieving relatives, and much of the template for an influential story formula is laid down. Gracious living and deplorable deeds go hand in hand,

and Cagney does something surprising with a grapefruit. With one foot in truth and the other in make believe, this is superior stuff.

White Heat – this fine piece of noir is Cagney at his best, in Raoul Walsh's hard hitting piece of classic crime drama. The worrying Freudian connection between Cody and Ma makes Cagney's unhinged, cruel gangster lead all the more perturbing.

The scene where Cody learns of Ma's death while he is in prison, was filmed without telling the extras (all real prisoners) what was going on. Many thought they were seeing James Cagney having a real life breakdown, so convincing was his acting. If you watch it again, have a look at some of the expressions of the people around him – real convicts who aren't sure how to react.

Cody turns increasingly wild and unpredictable, and the harsh, cold man he was at the start seems like a pussycat compared to how he ends up. The tension in this film is consistent and hard to ignore. This is a masterpiece, a genuinely hard hitting and powerful slice of noir. The ending would have to rank as one of the best ever.

Little Caesar – Edward G Robinson's grinching sourpuss face launched a thousand snarls as Rico, determined entrepreneur and not a man to be crossed.

Resentment, double crossing, irrational threats, power struggles, ambition and greed mark the knife of a character's rise to the top.

This influential performance clearly had as much of an impact on Pacino in *Scarface* as the original Howard Hawks movie did. His aggressive, resentful, ready to kill at the drop of a hat pride, combined with a low feral cunning show a side of gangsterdom that is both unattractive and compelling.

Apart from all the trailblazing gangster imagery this movie pioneered, it is worth seeing for Robinson's surly performance. The way he knits his eyebrows and glares makes Bogart look like a choirboy. No doubt the strength of this fine performance – not entirely matched by the rest of the film's quality – made a mark on tough guy actors that is still felt today.

The Maltese Falcon – this film defines the word 'classic.' If you've msissed it so far, I suggest keeping a good eye out. Bogart is at his leering, suspicious best, and Peter Lorre is sneeringly magnificent as an odious, unscrupulous agent of 'dark forces.'

The falcon in question is a gold statue made in the sixteenth century, and the model used has an air of opulence and intrigue. Aside from the vast fortune in gold, it represents a sense of the people involved – mysterious, powerful and capable of bringing great ruthlessness.

Reputedly based on Dashiell Hammett's own experience as a Pinkerton detective, he gave Sam Spade his own first name (jettisoned when he began a writing career) and a good deal of insight.

This novel was first published in 1930. Bogart's 1941 version was the third time it had been filmed, although the two previous productions had serious flaws. This was John Huston's first film, and while he pulls some of the punches from the novel's ending, Bogart plays Spade just as Hammett wrote it. In this movie his sneer is so huge you need a big screen to take in both corners at the same time. Wonderful.

Double Indemnity – this is a benchmark thriller for a number of reasons, but the chemistry between Fred MacMurray's opportunist insurance salesman and Barbara Stanwyck's smouldering, predatory femme fatale is intense. MacMurray's one sole gleam of intelligence is realising why he is being asked about insurance details – and he goes downhill from there.

Edward G Robinson makes MacMurray squirm by going over the details of the scheme, before realising he was talking to the "mastermind." Robinson has never been better than the dynamo of intelligence and commitment that slowly unravels the plot. The uneasy scenes the two share are a pleasure to watch, and the difference in height between them somehow makes MacMurray seem even more guilty.

Director Billy Wilder wrote the script with Raymond Chandler, and the whole film oozes quality. It deserves its lauded status and should be watched by anyone who wants to see a masterful example of how to wring as much pressure and tension from a situation as possible. MacMurray's performance is wonderful as he attempts to wriggle out of the noose he's in. It's an excellent film.

Dial M For Murder – one of Hitchcock's best, but a lot of critics have savaged its acting. Personally, I find it a riveting movie and the acting works superbly – there is more than a touch of ham on offer here, but the whole thing is entertaining and effective.

A former tennis pro decides to get rid of his wife, the delectable Grace Kelly. Having set her up to be murdered, exploiting an old friendship in the process, he then callously stands by and misleads her completely when the attempt goes wrong.

Part of Ray Milland's appeal here is the complete lack of feeling he exhibits, whilst perfectly going through the motions. The fact that he arranges to have dinner with his wife's lover at the time he arranged to have her killed says much about his cold mind – and his expression when she answers the phone is a picture.

North By Northwest – one of Cary Grant's most famous roles, this has so many great scenes it could be watched repeatedly just to see which parts haven't been used elsewhere. The plot is excessive and silly, but the pace of the movie and its thrills are more than enough to compensate.

For something that has so many plot holes, this film's undeniable tension is a major achievement of storytelling. It's an outstanding tribute to Hitchcock and his cast, and such a rewarding classic that I can't imagine anyone not enjoying it.

Dirty Harry – if this isn't Clint at his meanest, it's got to be pretty close. Brutal crimes, a brutal cop, a brutal criminal, a brutal gun, brutal sideburns, brutal sweaters – this isn't a gentle film. It is a groundbreaking slice of gritty, tense and involving crime fiction, and I defy anyone to be bored or uninvolved once the harsh, urban nightmare storyline gets going. As Harry wades through a world of sleaze to get his man, we see two ruthless, intensely focused people playing off each other.

If you haven't seen this, what're you using your eyeballs for?

Magnum Force – this worthy sequel somehow manages to outdo its predecessor for brutality. A neat reversal is that this time more cops are taking Harry's DIY approach to the court system, only to find Mr Callaghan getting in the way with all the confusion of a librarian leading a lynch mob.

Once more this is hard-nosed Dirty Harry fare, and again it's hard not to feel totally involved as all manner of crime takes place. As with the first, there is the tug of contradiction – how far can we understand and accept such excessive police measures? Its pedigree – written by the people who later helped *Apocalypse Now* and *The Deer Hunter* to the screen – assures us of some quality. This is another example of the genre, and it knows where all the gears are. For all it may be dismissed as a sequel, this stands as a strong thriller on its own.

Mean Streets – the film that first drew attention to Scorsese, a dazzling mix of colour, raw emotion and power that captured an energy not seen before. This high impact blend of street life, moralising and violence was set to a soundtrack of such great music that if the material had been any less stunning, it would have been a terrible waste.

De Niro and Kietel blaze across the screen with such conviction and swagger that the movie almost feels like a documentary. The by now familiar – but new in 1973 – visual style fits the material to perfection. The energetic camerawork adds a physical element here that gives the movie an added force that makes it breathtaking.

Having grown up around a variety of crime figures, and with a inquisitive, contemplative mind, Scorsese produced a potent mixture of moralising and greed in this punch in the face of a movie. *Mean Streets* was described by *The New Yorker's* Pauline Kael as having a "thicker textured rot" than ever seen before in American cinema. It's not hard to see how this developed into the harsh palette of *Taxi Driver* several years later.

Chinatown – if you've read this far you've hopefully seen a fair few ways in which this is an exemplary film. It's an all round winner that I can't recommend highly enough, but if asked for specific reasons I'd advise you watch it for how incredibly well judged it is. The positioning of all the required parts of the story is done with such skill and pace that the viewer is drawn in and finds their interest entwined with the lives on screen.

As with many investigations, we have the sleuth believing he is thoroughly in control of events, until he is so out of his depth it almost invites our sympathy. Nicholson's coarse but just private eye stands out as a good man because fundamentally he is, especially when compared with the levels of corruption he finds himself embroiled in. Faye Dunaway, far more knowing, far more intelligent, is a figure of great intrigue. When watching this, remember that the ending used is very different from the one in the original screenplay.

As a piece of period noir, it is a success on all fronts. A must see.

The Untouchables – this has very little to do with what really happened with Eliot Ness and Al Capone, but no matter. Kevin Costner's career best performance sees a clean cut man of integrity having to surround himself with a small group of incorruptables to take on a major crime syndicate.

Whilst that premise is as old as the hills, it is De Palma's grandiose style that makes the film work so well. There are fantastic performances across the board, and some fine setpieces, but the visual elegance is what leaves the strongest impression. Luckily this applies equally to the violence as it does the clothing and scenery, so the movie satisfies on many levels.

Ennio Morricone provided the score, which absolutely crowns the material, adding both real class and many emotional boosts. The Capone theme on its own radiates power, majesty and a sense of the formidable. De Niro wore silk boxers from Capone's own pantmaker to give his performance authenticity. I'm sure that made all the difference.

The Name of the Rose – this clever, intricate thriller departs from the norm in a number of key areas. First of all, most of the main characters have taken holy orders, which is a bit of a surprise. The atmosphere is of darkiness and dread, all among an order of monks in the fourteenth century, suspicious of at the least murder and at the most some foully unnatural practice.

As with some of the finest mysteries, the crime seems to be utterly baffling. A number of clerics are found dead, with blackened tongues. This puts people in mind of the diabolical. It's a fairly sinister detail today – nearly a thousand years ago such a thing would have been enough to induce hysteria.

This is a beautifully made movie with a collection of fine performances, including a prize turn from a young Christian Slater. The monastery used was twelfth century and gives a genuinely creepy feel, one cleverly exploited by the director.

King of New York – this has so much to recommend it, not least a killer performance from Christopher Walken as one of his best dead eyed murderers. His role of Frank White sees a man released from prison and determined to make good use of his freedom, taking back what was his (and more so) and making some impressively selfless pledges for his wealth. It's a story of a hard nut sociopath reborn, more ruthless than before, and also more dedicated.

The rest of the cast is seriously impressive. Laurence Fishburne provides adept, homicidal support as a loyal triggerman, Steve Buscemi makes a characteristically excellent appearance as a narcotics chemist and shooter, with Wesley Snipes and David Caruso playing impetuous young cops determined not to stand idly by while White and his gang brutally flout the law.

Victor Argo stands out as the mentor cop, attempting to put White back inside while at the same time restraining the younger cops who are drawn to vigilante action. The imagery is astounding, with especially fine cinematography. This is a hard hitting thriller, and very fully recommended – Abel Ferrera at his best.

Goodfellas – this is a stunning, powerful and intoxicating film. From its sharp opening to the last image of Joe Pesci unloading his gun straight into the camera, this is a masterful example of everything that's good about crime films.

Plenty has been said about this elsewhere, but if anyone doubts the quality of this, all I can say is watch it. If you've watched it and still think this is lacking, then I hope you get better soon.

If I could recommend only one item on this list, it would be Goodfellas.

Wild At Heart – this isn't directly a crime flick and yet in an odd way it is. Certainly it could count as a thriller, and there's plenty of lawbreaking going on, so that's all fair enough. What makes this work so well is that routine noir elements are taken, kicked up a gear and combined with David Lynch's breathtaking, surreal imagery.

A bizarre cast and eccentric, extreme visuals make this a memorable and fiercely enjoyable movie. Nicholas Cage gives a fine turn as a bad Elvis type parole jumper, with Laura Dern as his crazy younger lover, along with extensive baggage. All of the performances in this movie really hit the mark, particularly Willem Dafoe's mad, ratty criminal (who meets an astoundingly impressive end) and his lousy teeth.

This has more than a few elements in common with the Coen Brothers' movies. The gargoyles, grotesques and badasses peppering this story at every turn just add to the flavour.

Pulp Fiction – one of the definitive movies of the 90's. Iconic is the word for this fantastic crime spree of a piece of storytelling. Famously, three storylines weave in and out of each other, and time is adjusted to suit the impetus of the narrative.

The elements that made *Reservoir Dogs* so compelling – the brutal violence, laconic swearing, priceless soundtrack and fluid cinematography – are included here, with extras. Whilst both movies ooze cool at every pore, *Pulp Fiction* has Samuel L Jackson and Uma Thurman, not to mention a mystical strand of plot juggling that baffles and intrigues.

Incidentally, in terms of chronology, Bruce Willis driving off on Zed's chopper is the last event of the film. I think. And the briefcase contains Marcellus Wallace's supply of Toblerone. Or his soul. Or something like that.

The Usual Suspects – this is another head scratching piece of cinematic brilliance. A devilish mastermind is at work, exploiting human nature, tantalising blind spots and menacing the imagination.

But enough about the scriptwriter. I gather this fine movie was made due to the tenacity of several of its stars, who all agreed it was a great idea and they wanted to be part of it. Lots of people's people were talking to other people's people about this, who all discussed it with other people, so it's amazing the ending surprised anyone.

Last But Not Least ...

Seriously though, this is an amazingly rich and entertaining film. There's such a lot going on. Moreover, in 16 countries it is legal to kill anyone who spoils the ending.

The Big Lebowski – okay, it's not a straightforward thriller. But it does have kidnapping, missing toes, bizarre anarchists, robbery, rug pissing and some howlingly funny moments. If this doesn't entertain you, I don't know what will.

The aspect of this film that I find hugely impressive is the way the violence and confrontations still impress despite all the silly, laid back stoner humour. John Goodman's supporting turn is priceless and I can see why the Coen brothers have so much time for him.

London film critic Alexander Walker described this film as a "shaggy dog story out for a walk," and maybe that's fair enough, but it's great fun. Also, if you've ever wondered what would happen if someone wrapped up an UZI and then dropped it, then this is the film for you.

No Country For Old Men – much of this is close to perfect, as a strong tale builds up over a series of compelling dramatic events. The characters are all strictly believable and what unfolds does so with a strong sense of inevitability. It's a tense, gripping film that proves massively involving.

A big question with this film concerns the ending, as bizarre as that may sound. I still can't decide what I think of it. The great lines and stunning all round performances make for a measured and accomplished thriller. This is a masterful film.

The Departed – more Scorsese but so what? This is a clever, compelling film and the last really outstanding gangster movie I saw. As with *Goodfellas*, it has its roots in real people. Again, the soundtrack is amazing, and accompanies incredibly stylised, hard hitting violence. Also, Ray Winstone gives Jack Nicholson a run for his money in terms of who has the most celluloid cool. Astounding – just watch it.

Casino Royale – a thundering reinjection of noir credentials sends the Bond franchise steaming forward, not just coughing politely as things get sillier. The well considered opening, Bond earning his stripes as a killer (in studied black and white) reminds us that here is someone with a brutal job, not first and foremost a playboy.

The action was made grittier and more realistic, and it's clear that massive effort went into making the film as hectic as possible while retaining credibility. The stunts received particular acclaim.

No bone is left uncrunched as Bond headbutts his way into the 21st century. The end product had wallop and style and took in $600m at the box office, enough to keep the bean counters happily shelling out for more scaffolding and tuxedos.

Last But Not Least ...

A great many other outstanding movies could be recommended here – and quite a few real classics haven't been mentioned, including *The Godfather, Bullitt* and *The French Connection* – but there has to be a limit. If some particular favourite isn't here, please do bear in mind this isn't supposed to be an exhaustive list.

Recommended Crime Books

All of these books are fine examples of the genre, and most have more than a touch of masterful ability about them. They are all strongly recommended for a number of reasons, and I would earnestly suggest that people read them, if only for the entertainment.

The Hound of the Baskervilles by Sir Arthur Conan-Doyle

This intense and ferocious mystery has amazing atmosphere. I can still recall how, when I first read it, I was looking up regularly – just to make sure things were okay. The book's suspicion and sense of darkness are infectious, and it becomes incredibly gripping very quickly.

The plot is fiendishly good, skillfully using a number of pieces of superstition and fear to inject a sense of unease in the reader. Apart from the many strands of intricate puzzle that help grip our attention, Conan-Doyle cleverly draws on our worst suspicions about the paranormal, making sinister use of old folk legends.

In addition to Holmes' unusual methods and personal conduct, the villain scores top points for his diabolical ideas. Wonderful. If you only read one book from this list, *The Hound of the Baskervilles* would be my nomination.

The Valley of Fear by Sir Arthur Conan-Doyle

The second Holmes book I'm recommending is also a novel, although many of the short stories are excellent. This story has a terrible crime at the offset, with a corpse shot faceless. Holmes, called in to investigate, finds a scene of intrigue that rivals any of his cases.

Much of the story is told in the form of a flashback, but not one being recounted by a narrator. It is described as any current day event, and concerns a sect called the Scowrers, a secret society of criminals rather like a nineteenth century Mafia.

A new man arrives in town, a fierce looking individual who claims to be on the run. When he presents himself at the Scowrer lodge, he has references with their organisation and a knowledge of their ways and customs. After his local initiation, he is welcomed into their fold and immediately given criminal work to perform.

The tension and of this book work incredibly well. Holmes is forced to work hard to discover the truth behind the event at the start of the novel. We are shown a fine insight into the mindset of a community in terror, and the twist at the end is a fine example of the storyteller's art.

I, The Jury by Mickey Spillane

Mike Hammer, Spillane's hard boiled private dick, is in his element here. Even though this was released in 1947, it hits a number of buttons that apparently belong to more recent fare. It certainly isn't restrained in any way.

The femme fatale is a psychotherapist, sexually voracious and murderous – more than slightly reminiscent of Sharon Stone's *Basic Instinct* character. The killings are sadistic. A one armed war veteran (a friend of Hammer's who lost his arm saving his life in WWII) – is shot in the stomach, his murderer watching the agonising slow death he endures.

The other crimes involved also seem modern, and again seem very similar to some much more recent thrillers. Drug use and a ring of exotic prostitutes intersect with tremendous greed and ruthlessness. Mike Hammer is faced with a desperate woman (who just happens to be smouldering hot), a murdered friend, suspects galore and a thirst for retribution, all of which power this hugely enjoyable story.

It's .45s and bourbon all round in this fine piece of intrigue. This was the first of the Mike Hammer novels, and it broke new ground that continues to influence crime stories today.

The Ingredients Of A Good Thriller

Goldfinger by Ian Fleming

One of the best Bond novels, this is both a compelling spy thriller and an expert crime tale. We begin with Bond, the suave, well travelled hard man, reflecting on his last case, in which he killed a man with his bare hands and broke a heroin ring. He's musing over this with a well earned drink when an acquaintance recognises him and pleads for his help. In this way Bond first encounters Goldfinger, a hugely wealthy man who is also a petty cheat – and soon proves himself a killer.

Bond is drawn into the world of a genuine meglomaniac and one of the best villains ever. One of my favourite scenes is when our famous spy is present at a meeting of top criminals. To make his ambitious plans work, Goldfinger recruits gang leaders from across American crime networks. The power and influence of the man, being unafraid as he is to kill major underworld figures, is an impressive combination.

It also contains one of the best lines going, from one gang leader to Goldfinger: "Mister, you're the greatest thing to happen to crime since Cain invented murder and used it on Abel." Superb.

The Grifters by Jim Thompson

This ride into the life of petty crime is immediately kick started with the information that the main character has received a fatal injury – and a timer is set on his life. We're then drawn into his world as we discover how this was inflicted, and, as with many Jim Thompson books, the details about the sleazy side of life are excellent.

Thompson lived a wayward existence, to put it mildly. He started off with surprisingly hard edged acts at a very tender age. His crime fiction is tinged with massive amounts of authenticity, detail that came from first hand experience and his natural aptitude for such things.

For those who – like most of us – live in a way far removed from the professional criminal, it is a fascinating slice of an underclass way of living. This was the first Jim Thompson book I read, and the type of book that gets devoured as quickly as possible.

The Killer Inside Me by Jim Thompson

There's harsh and there's harsh, and this elaborate first person narrative is tough as nails, barbed wire harsh. For a book containing very little actual violence, the impact it has is considerable and a tribute to the author's expertise.

The friendly tone of Lou Ford, this apparently warm man, makes his deeds even harder to take. This superbly considered piece of writing carries us along with a sociopath as he goes about his life and crimes.

The wonderful storytelling takes us right into his mind. We see his warped reasoning, bizarre approach to his own actions and, most disturbingly, his feelings of betrayal and being cheated when he finds that one of his victims has survived! This is what the term 'hard boiled' was designed for.

Carlito's Way and *After Hours* by Edwin Torres

These two great books were amalgamated into the script for the De Palma movie, one of the best gangster films of the 90's, that saw Pacino and Sean Penn on top form. Most of the events in the movie are from *After Hours* (which, like the adaptation, begins with Carlito's surprise release from jail), but the tone of the character owes a lot to the first book.

Written in a street smart, first person, Puerto Rico meets New York narrative, we have an intelligent, hip, ruthless and likeable criminal in Carlito Brigante. A hustler and opportunist turned major league heroin dealer, he has the instincts and loyalties of a "neighbourhood guy" despite having been rich enough to have a gangster's entourage. As he wryly notes at one point, "It cost me fifty balloons just to get my hair cut."

He meets the mafia, some glorious women and takes his idiosyncratic, preternaturally aware self on some great ups and downs. The descriptions of loyalties, duels, street life and seduction are masterful. Torres used to work as an NYC judge in the night court hearings, and it shows. This is very fine work.

The Choirboys by Joseph Wambaugh

Five very different pairs of cops pound the same beat. They are all very different people, and their approaches vary hugely. After their shift, they meet up to swap views and stories, to get loaded and laid. They call this 'choir practice.'

The story is full of realistic detail and is told in a powerful way with words punchy enough to make the reader lose teeth. The book is hilarious too, and the nicknames cops have for each other and their varying ways of fixing themselves, both on and off duty, make for fascinating reading.

Wambaugh spent 14 years with the LAPD and shows an insider's eye here. He captures so many different angles of the police officer's take on people, society and crime that it would have had to come from close, first hand experience as well as a top writer's eye for detail.

Brighton Rock by Graham Greene (spoiler warning)

Guilt, duty and religious fixations have a lot to answer for, especially when taken to extremes. That is exactly where 17 year old gang leader Pinkie takes them. Thoroughly convinced that he is destined to burn eternally, he sees nothing to be lost in killing, burning, slicing and robbing all who displease him.

That is how this cruel, twisted soul ends up at the helm of a crew of Brighton gangsters. These extortionists see a ruthlessness and determination in Pinkie that makes him a leader, even if his psychotic fixations give all of them pause.

This fine novel of sin and retribution reads like high literature, with a precise and detailed style, but with the compulsion and content of a top thriller. We have victims, dupes, accomplices and avengers – particularly the latter in Ida, a good and determined woman whose basic decency undoes a vicious criminal. Pinkie certainly burns horribly at the end.

For Ida – sensuous, kindly, tenacious and oddly childish – Pinkie is an incarnation of evil. The novel ends with an uncomfortable scene of soul searching in a confessional. For this good woman, the proximity of such sin is enough to damn at least part of her – her emotions.

The Godfather by Mario Puzo

This is one of the best pieces of popular fiction I have ever read, and spans a vast amount of time over several different cultures. It is one of those rare books that can make you immediately understand a scene and its setting, and regularly throws up insights into lifestyles and people in general that both stun and illuminate.

For all the brilliance of Coppola's adaptation, the book really contains more. It is a fine example of how a dynasty is founded, and presents such plausible motives for all the people concerned that the corruption inherent in the family's affairs becomes much more readily understandable.

Part of the book's massive impact comes from the casual brutality of the characters, who order deaths and immensely savage beatings with the same regard that an accountant pays to figures – important pieces of business, but not a source of emotion.

It is a great skill to be able to span so many families, and so many different perspectives so quickly. Puzo includes that many differing approaches to life in his characters that after finishing the book, it is tempting to immediately read it again, both for pleasure and to absorb more of the incredible level of detail. This is a fine book to be savoured.

Get Shorty by Elmore Leonard

A great deal could be said about Leonard's mastery of the crime genre. His books have been adapted regularly over his five decade career. Often the finished product that hit the screen bore little resemblance to the book he wrote, but *Get Shorty* is one of the honourable exceptions.

This book works so well because it contains many diverse parts that gel together. Loan sharks, movie stars, B-movie directors, scream queens, petty crooks, coke barons and sadistic gang bosses don't have a lot in common. In Elmore Leonard's hands, however, they do.

Making such apparently odd parts gel as naturally as this is a measure of rare skill. The language fits perfectly and on every page the reader is completely at home with the characters and events. In terms of how to make a piece of fiction work, this would have to count as a rare example of complete, apparently effortless success.

Strip Tease by Carl Hiassen

Drunken congressman making fools of themselves in strip clubs will always be entertaining. The full complement of sleazy vote grabbers in this fine, funny page turner gives great value for money. Whether they are full bore buffoons whose lives are thoroughly turned over, or just one trick window dressing roles who underscore how bent this part of the system is, the entertainment value they afford is considerable.

For the main character, throw in the gorgeous Erin, stripper extraordinaire (who can actually dance), suffering problems from her ex, custody issues with her daughter and a load of horny politicos drooling after her, and you have a great story.

The novel could easily be considered political satire, not that anyone associated with Capitol Hill has ever been corrupt, drunk or prone to fascinations with exotic dancers! This book is very funny and surprisingly gripping. The movie was a huge disappointment, although Burt Reynolds made a fine drooling fool of himself in a great supporting role.

Capone by Lawrence Bergreen

This incredibly detailed biography of the world's foremost gangster includes swathes of interesting information. There is not only a good deal about this infamous figure that fascinates, but also about the era itself. Capone, for example, was estimated to have between 250 and 400 people killed a year, and was constantly paranoid about his own men turning on him.

The most memorable detail for me was the way this outlandish meglomaniac would buy a newspaper with a $50 bill. During the Depression, this was a small fortune. Then, when the quaking vendor would apologise for not being able to offer change from such a huge sum, Capone would growl "Who the hell asked you for change?"

Without A Badge by Jerry Speziale with Mark Seal

This incredible account of a New York DEA agent going undercover with some sincerely dangerous cocaine barons is gripping and intriguing. His descriptions of his regular policework and then his extra special assignment present the reader with a good deal of insight into large investigations.

One of the most impressive parts is the way Speziale describes his emotions, and the way he presents the stark terror of some situations. A good deal of thought provoking reality makes this memoir tense and involving. Some of the details of the seizures and arrests do sound extremely far fetched, but not so much as the personalities of some of the criminals.

The cumulative effect of his ultra high stress work is a form of breakdown, which is both inevitable and fascinating. Anyone wanting to read an authoritative view of life as an undercover cop, and see some of the bizarre details that present themselves, should look at this.

Red Dragon by Thomas Harris

This first glimpse of Hannibal Lector achieved a feat few other crime books manage – it frightened the readers. This tale of a demonic killer details his fascination with the lunar cycle, William Blake and the importance of wiping out entire families. The best investigator to catch this fiend before another family dies is a retired, scarred cop with plenty of baggage. Oh, and Hannibal Lector starts tugging at our demons for the first time.

One of the most impressive things in this novel is the sparse way the graphic crimes are revealed. The reader is teased with the murders, with aspects of the grisly acts being revealed slowly enough to both tantalise and repel. Surprisingly, the writer's explanations behind the killer's evil deeds enrich our picture of what is going on without in any way lessening our revulsion at the horror at his acts.

If the amount of breathless tension a book contains is an indication of its quality – and in this area, I'm sure it is – then this is a masterpiece. The atmosphere of dread is very strong, and the hideous crimes sufficiently powerful to get a reaction even among today's audiences, who have been exposed to some very graphic fare.

The Silence of the Lambs by Thomas Harris

This famous, celebrated sequel is by no means a pale repetition of the formula that made *Red Dragon* such a powerful read. While we have another serial killer committing atrocities (again of a new and horrifying nature), it is the tenderness of the young, vulnerable detective and the enhanced role for Hannibal Lector that act as the accelerators here.

Part of Thomas Harris' great skill with these stories is the way he produces crimes that are both unbelievably vile as well as completely compelling. Here the monster at loose is doing bizarre and vile things, and we find ourselves drawn in because the crimes are so gruesomely intriguing.

Each part of the material is used to maximise the story's impact. Entwining Clarice Starling's troubled upbringing with the fate of the woman at the bottom of Buffalo Bill's dreadful prison is a fine, intelligent touch and helps humanise extreme and disturbing fare.

Donnie Brasco by Joseph D. Pistone

Another undercover agent's true tale of bravery and nerve shredding experiences, this time looking at day to day existence with the New York mafia. The observations he makes provide fascinating reading for anyone curious about such a way of life. Whilst it made for a very good film, I'd strongly recommend reading this as the author's touches – his agent's eye for details – are intriguing and thought provoking.

The film adaptation – complete with stunning cast – covers much of the change in personality this agent underwent. His exposure to thugs and murderers changed his moods and attitudes, making him difficult to live with and volatile in his private life.

The level of immersion required to make undercover work effective is astounding, and the first hand experiences related here are riveting. Pistone's refusal to be intimidated (not an easy feat in the face of mafia retribution, I imagine) is astounding, and there is much to be admired in his approach. The man Al Pacino played (Lefty Two Guns – what a great name for a gangster!) has sworn revenge. The mob responded with a $500,000 price on his head, the sign of a job well done.

Last But Not Least ...

The Hitman Diaries by Danny King

Professional assassins have a status that proper culture has exploited for all it's worth, but few people stop and consider their lives as ordinary people. Danny King does just that in this exciting, brutal but somehow light-hearted book.

This starts well – a date ending in several impromptu executions, never a good sign – and includes a lot of details about the everyday aspects of the man's life. It has some beautifully considered ideas, and the writer makes it all work.

It also has a lot of entertaining violence, a manipulative boss, a worrying student assassin and a good deal of heartbreak for our neurotic contract killer. The scenes in which he drinks his guilt away, having mailed himself the key to his gun safe (to prevent suicide), show an inventive approach to 'professional' difficulties.

Slayground by Philip Caveney

A lot of people find the idea of feral, dangerous children unnerving. This is understandable, as the issue poses so many questions – how far would you go to restrain a child? As what age do you begin to understand right from wrong? Could a child with a gun conceivably comprehend the enormity of taking a life?

This book exploits these fears expertly. Finn, the underage, undersized leader of a teenage gang, spearheads his friends' descent into peril and deep criminality. Finn's home life contains many less than desirably elements, and his mind is full of gangster imagery and an unwillingness to just lie down and let life crush him.

Sadly, Finn and his friends find themselves far from the strong, caring guidance they need. Led astray by the dope dealing equivalent of Fagin, he finds himself armed, hunted and with his back to the wall.

This book pounds along and has a surprisingly human eye for the people involved. The exploration of violence is top notch, and *Slayground* contains one of the best descriptions of automatic gunfire I've ever read. *Strip Jack Naked*, by the same author, is also strongly recommended, and contains a genuinely sickening description of a kneecapping. Fine stuff.

LA Confidential by James Ellroy

This fast paced and extensive thriller packs a good meaty punch. It begins with a fantastically written piece of gunplay, which showcases Ellroy's fierce writing as well as anything. We then proceed to the situation that frames the book's events – the LAPD celebrating Christmas.

Bud White – thuggish hater of wife beaters – is molesting a parolee after he returns home and starts with the domestic abuse again. He is balanced out by Ed Exley, goody two-shoes war hero who intends to rise within the police ranks with considerable speed.

When the plot takes off, as it does with great force, we see a brutal tableau. A child mutilating serial killer, a pimp with movie star lookalike clientele, a theme park based on corruption, crooked police, a gang leader in jail, a cop with two innocent kills tormenting him, graphic porn, a raped Mexican national – it's cheerful stuff all right, but the Christmas spirit is somehow lacking.

Anyone wanting to see how a book can be made exciting and powerful should read this. The story progresses with the crushing progress of a steamroller combined with Ferrari handling. The details and fast observations set up scenes of great power, and whilst the film was amazing, this truly tops it in every respect.

American Tabloid by James Ellroy

The mystery around JFK's assassination has never been satisfactorily explained to the public. Here Ellroy produces a plausible, fictional re-enactment of the events in Dallas, and what led up to them.

The players are an odd bunch – a gigantic, brutal killer and bagman, two FBI agents, one corrupt, one (initially) a straight player, a portrayal of Howard Hughes even more grotesque than the reality, Jimmy Hoffa, Frank Sinatra (portrayed as an egotistical monster) and various mob figures.

A number of historical events, including the Bay of Pigs fiasco, are drawn upon. The lives of Ellroy's characters are grimed with sleaze; the best of them is certainly no saint. The violence is again fast and brutal, full of vicious invention and harsh detail.

One of the parts I liked best about this novel was the way it charged like a mad bull into the Kennedy legend, sparing nobody in the presentation of a corrupt dynasty and its effect on America. The entwined story regarding the characters credited with the dirty deeds is a masterful piece of drama.

I could go on recommending, but you get the idea. As with the list of films, apologies for all the omissions.

Afterword

Conclusion – The Essentials

This Is The Vital Stuff

People are interested in thrillers because of justice and mystery. Someone pays for their crime – that keeps us watching. Finding out what happened in a confusing or compelling situation – that does it, too. People love intrigue.

This requires a situation, characters and a setting.

Situation

The plot chapter deals with the seven deadly sins, but greed, jealousy and revenge are all good starting points. They work very easily.

I have something you want – you rob me
You have something I want – I rob you
One of us gets vengeful – we take action

It's helpful if we think of as many interchangeable parts as possible.

To put that in an easy situation, I have just inherited a gold statue. You don't think that's fair, as a distant relative left it to me as the only kin. We work together and you think I don't deserve it.

So ... you break into my house, only you get the wrong house. It's next door, and an elderly couple has discovered you. In the panic, one has a heart attack. The other rushes at you. In self defence, you restrain them – now you have two bodies. You rush off.

The next day at work, I tell you of the horrible thing that happened in the night. I'm spooked by it. So are you, but for different reasons.

Then you find a blackmail note. Somebody saw you. They want thousands for their silence, or you face disgrace and jail. The only source of this money is my gold statue. You now have to steal it.

Plus, you suspect that it's me blackmailing you. Something in our past means I hold a grudge, and I want you to break in, so I can trap you rather than go to the police without an airtight case.

Now, that deals with greed, jealousy and revenge. That might seem a bit haphazard, but something to do with one of the big three is used in all thrillers. They're just used in different ways, like musicians play chords differently.

That covers the basics. A plot can be as complex as you like. Once the basic is set up, things can be given more intrigue.

Sub Plots

Having another strand of plot going on adds extra interest. It also means you can throw in more crimes, more intrigue, more sleaze or whatever butters your toast.

So ... I bumped off my distant relative and forged the will. Or maybe I fabricated the whole thing because the bank has tried to foreclose, or my crooked business partners want their money back, or my wife's threatened to leave me, or I need to stall a blackmailer.

Maybe the neighbours only died because they were exhausted after their poker night. Perhaps you broke into the wrong house because you really have a split personality and don't work with me at all. Maybe you need the money to silence an outraged lover even before the blackmail.

Basically, extra vices are interesting. They needn't be graphic, unless you want that. Also, what you hint at can be a lot more powerful than what we actually see.

The best thing is to get people asking questions. Like, how can this get worse? Will it get really desperate? How do they get caught?

Characters

Firstly, we have the main character. This needs to be someone the audience looks up to in some form. Either they are smart or strong, or an appealing anti-hero.

We also need someone to be suspicious of, and either a character to hate or a criminal – perhaps unknown throughout most of the thriller – whose identity is intriguing to us.

Love interest is always good. Any characters that add suspicion, or tension, or fear, work wonderfully. The next time you watch or read a thriller, try to notice when the really interesting stuff is being included. That can be difficult to notice, but be aware of your own reactions. Something in the story has shifted – are you tense now? Fascinated? Would it take an earthquake to tear your attention away? That's what you're aiming at delivering.

Setting

Where are you comfortable? What do you know? Where do you imagine the events taking place? A lot of great stories are set in places the author knows well. Equally, some people write about times or places they have never experienced first hand.

The important thing is to consider if you can make it work. A lot of thrillers use their setting as an implicit part of the story, others barely make notice. Many great thrillers could have been set anywhere, provided that the requisite type of people are there.

Decide for yourself, of course. The chapter on settings will help here.

Audience Motivation

The biggest question to ask yourself is, Why does anyone give a damn? Making a crime personal always helps – a loved one killed, a dear friend brought down, or just some generally heinous act that requires payback. Anything that has to be followed up in the audience's mind is what you're aiming at.

People are attracted to a number of thriller elements. A mystery, some sleaze, a crime of passion, the prospect of a good shoot out or car chase, the resolution of some great enigma – these are the currency of thrillers. Deliver here and the audience is your friend.

Am I Underlining Too Much?

In terms of giving clues, introducing people and so forth, judging how to put things in for the reader or audience to take in can take some doing. On the one hand, you want them to notice. On the other, when does spoonfeeding start? Consider this example:

The Rock steals a bold move over the audience. Right at the start, when Ed Harris is explaining his motives to his wife's grave, on the stone, just above her name it reads 'His wife.' Quite a cheeky move, but it doesn't spoil the movie. I certainly didn't notice at the cinema, not until it was repeated on TV, and there is was, blatant as it gets. Full marks for nerve, and it doesn't get in the way.

Judging the audience is important. Given what works so well in *The Rock*, maybe it was considered okay to take a short cut.

In any case, ticket offices at multiplexes don't get razed to the ground because the Saturday night audience found the exposition obvious. And if it works, well, fair enough.

The Usual Suspects contains a shot in which the word 'handgun' appears, in bold print, in an envelope right by Kevin Spacey. If this is some subtle way of jacking up tension, or relates to some intricate behind the scenes plot matter, I don't know. But probably the sub-conscious eye notices this. I had seen the film several times before realising it was on screen.

The name of the game here is success. Don't worry about being too obvious or too subtle. The first time you write something, give yourself the benefit of the doubt. After the first draft is completed, get some feedback and decide if your decision or device works.

If in doubt, go for it and worry later. You can always alter it!

Acknowledgements

David Griffith and George Lear for being the first people to read it, and David Griffith again for editing it.

Sean O'Callaghan for his always inspirational ideas and Pat Wallwork for her helpful comments.

Kate Coley for providing more focus.

Catherine and Cornelius Mawby for their enthusiasm.

Joe Castle for being sure this didn't exist (kidding!).

Mark Coley, Simon Bestwick and Guy Couzens-Howard for consistently valuable film chat.

Coming soon ...

The Ingredients Of A Good Horror
by Chris Wood

Horror is always popular, and the last ten years have only seen an increase in this permanent favourite. Most people love ghost stories, tales of the supernatural and matters of murder.

If you're writing in this area, or are just interested, *The Ingredients Of A Good Horror* is for you.

This book looks at a wide variety of myths, superstitions, maniacs, curses, ghouls, monsters and ghosts. Easy to follow and full of useful information, this book breaks down the conventions of these stories in an entertaining and accessible way.

Imaginary creatures of the dark are discussed alongside real life nightmares, and the genre is considered in a way that appeals to writers and fans alike.

Coming 2009 from LDB Publishing

Coming soon ...

Sherlock Holmes and the Underpants of Death
by Chris Wood

Legendary detective Sherlock Holmes is a byword for intelligence and efficiency. Not any more. Detailing some of his less famous exploits, including the infamous drive by shittings of 1894, this rare volume covers a side of Holmes scarcely seen by the public: the real one.

Only this collection reveals the the mystery of the lingering stench, how Professor Moriarty didn't die and the truth behind the sinister Underpants of Death, a tale to freeze the blood and rapidly unblock the colon.

Coming 2009 from LDB Publishing

About The Author

Chris Wood is a writer and journalist from Manchester, England. He has written for a wide variety of publications and has a broad range of teaching experience.

The Ingredients Of A Good Thriller is his first book.

Breinigsville, PA USA
19 November 2009
227871BV00001B/54/P